# BEHIND THE GREEN MONSTER

## BY BILL BALLOU

Ambassador Books, Inc.
Worcester • Massachusetts

Acknowledgement is made to the *Worcester Telegram & Gazette* in which the story "The Red Seat" was originally published on September 21, 2003.

The Publisher wishes to thank the *Worcester Telegram & Gazette* for permission to use the cover photo of Opening Day at Fenway Park, April 11, 2005, where the 2004 World Series banner was unveiled.

*Library of Congress Cataloging-in-Publication Data*

Ballou, Bill, 1952-
  Behind the green monster / by Bill Ballou.
    p. cm.
  ISBN 1-929039-32-8 (pbk.)
  1.  Boston Red Sox (Baseball team)--History. 2.  Baseball players--United States--Biography. I. Title.

  GV875.B62B35 2005
  796.357'640974461--dc22

                                        2005030964

Published in the United States by Ambassador Books, Inc.
91 Prescott Street, Worcester, Massachusetts 01605
(800) 577-0909

*Printed in the United States of America.*

For current information about all titles from Ambassador Books, Inc., visit our website at: www.ambassadorbooks.com.

# Dedication

*To Debbie, for all of the evenings watching legion games in Amherst; to my mother and father, for letting me stay up to watch Dick Gernert bat; to Abby, for Seattle and San Francisco; and Mary, for Minneapolis and Atlanta; and Billy, for Chicago, Detroit and Toronto; and Rachael, for the eternal promise of next year.*

# Contents

# Acknowledgements

Nowhere is the "Everything I needed to know, I learned in kindergarten" theory more true than with covering major league baseball on a regular basis.

I started covering the Red Sox in 1987 and within a week's time went from thinking I knew everything there was to know to realizing I knew nothing at all.

During that first confusing year, I was most fortunate to meet several people who threw me life preservers whenever they saw my head disappear beneath the waves, which was often. Included on that list are Steve Krasner and the late Art Turgeon of the *Providence Journal*; Nick Cafardo, then of the *Quincy Patriot Ledger*; and Joe Giuliotti and Mike Shalin of the *Boston Herald*.

Also in 1987, I became acquainted with Joe Morgan, then the Red Sox' third base coach. He is treated kindly in this book, and with good reason. He remains the most knowledgeable baseball man I have ever met, as well as the most honest one I have ever met in, or out of, the world of sports.

Traveling baseball beat writers are a strange hybrid of competitor and companion. The best of both worlds inhabit the Boston beat. From the past and present, that list includes my co-workers over the years, Paul Jarvey and Phil O'Neill from the *Telegram & Gazette*; Sean McAdam of the *Providence Journal*; Tony Massarotti, Mike

Silverman, Jeff Horrigan, Karen Guregian and Steve Buckley of the *Boston Herald*; Sean Horgan of the *Hartford Courant*; Larry Whiteside, Dan Shaughnessy, Steve Fainaru, Bob Hohler, Gordon Edes and Chris Snow of the *Boston Globe*; Dave Heuschkel and Paul Doyle of the *Hartford Courant*; Dave Borges of the *Journal-Register* papers; and Seth Livingstone of the *Patriot-Ledger*.

At home games, I have enjoyed the company of Charles Scoggins of the *Lowell Sun*; Howard Ulman and Jimmy Golen of the Associated Press; Mike Fine of the *Patriot-Ledger*; Alan Greenwood of the *Nashua Telegraph*; Win Bates, Ken Lechtanski and Bob Stern of the *Brockton Enterprise*; Art Davidson and Lenny Megliola of the *Middlesex Daily News*; John Tomase of the *Lawrence Eagle-Tribune*; Joe McDonald and Paul Kenyon of the *Providence Journal*; and Ron Chimelis and Gary Brown of the *Springfield Republican*.

My thanks to my publisher, Gerry Goggins, for thinking my idea for a book was worth pursuing, and a former partner in writing, Cynthia Amsden, for thinking that a commercial book was worth pursuing at all. Also, at the *Telegram & Gazette*, editors such as Jim Connolly, Linc McKie, Bill Clew, John Widdison, Bud Barth, Dave Nathan, Dave Greenslit, Dave Nordman, and Mark Henderson; and co-workers like Henry Landress; the late Al Whitmarsh; Tim Murphy, Ken Powers, Jen Toland, Rich Garven, Paul Morano, Richie Lewis, Bill Doyle, John Conceison, Josh Bousquet, Jim Wilson, Brendan McGrail, Chris Christo, and Bill Fortier; as well as the bosses—Bruce Bennett, Harry Whitin and Leah Lamson—none of whom ever told me what, or what not, to write.

From the very old days, Mike deSherbinin of the late, wonderful, *Amherst Record* gave me my first real job in newspapers, and John Bart never stopped being a fan.

Thank you all, again.

# The Day the World Changed
## February 26, 2002

HISTORY IS OFTEN MADE IN WHISPERS, AS IT WAS IN FORT MYERS, Florida on the windy morning of February 26, 2002 when the Boston Red Sox took their first step towards winning the 2004 World Series.

The venerable American League franchise had new owners-elect—John Henry, Larry Lucchino and Tom Werner—who were due to pass papers on the sale the next day, officially bringing to an end the nearly 70 years of incessant misery and occasional delight that had marked the Tom Yawkey Era.

Yawkey had owned the team from 1933 until his death in 1976. He was a benign, indulgent despot and his passing had given rise to a jumble of administrations, all of them with one notable characteristic in common.

Incompetence. The Red Sox may as well have been Paraguay in how they were run.

At various times the Red Sox were owned, or at least operated, by Yawkey's widow, Jean; a former backup catcher, Haywood Sullivan; the team's one-time trainer, Buddy Leroux; and a former accounting instructor at Boston College, John Harrington.

From the time Yawkey died in the summer of 1976 through the morning of February 26, 2002, the Red Sox had appeared in the World Series only once.

Henry and his partners had entered into an agreement to buy the Red Sox just before Christmas 2001, but the paperwork was being done back in Boston as he arrived at spring training, 2002. The early weeks of spring training are held at the team's minor-league complex at the end of Edison Avenue in Fort Myers, a couple of miles down the road from City of Palms Park. It was here that Henry arrived on that otherwise unremarkable morning in late February.

That he was there was significant of itself. His predecessor, John Harrington, had become something of a Howard Hughes as the years went by. He was seen in public less and less. Then, when he was spotted, always seemed to have a plastic bag full of dry cleaning slung over his shoulder. Harrington's one Red Sox social event was the annual visit of Boston College, his alma mater, to City of Palms Park for an early spring training game. Otherwise, he avoided daylight like a termite.

On this morning, Harrington still officially ran the team, so Henry was there, but not quite yet in charge. The facility was buzzing with activity as players went about the serious business of warming up and fans went about the equally serious business of chasing down autographs and getting pictures snapped of them with their arms around Pedro Martinez, Jason Varitek, Nomar Garciaparra—hey, Rey Sanchez, you got a second?—anyone wearing a Boston uniform.

For everyone but the players and fans, though, the atmosphere on Edison Avenue was anything but business as usual. For the front office people, for the manager, for the general manager, for the coaches, for the scouts, it was as if they were all defendants standing in awful anticipation as the jury walked in with a verdict.

Henry, in a windbreaker and his standard wide-brimmed hat, walked towards one of the back diamonds and made his move as the

Sox prepared to take live batting practice—where big-league hitters bat against their big-league pitcher teammates—for the first time in the spring. He noticed the usual horde of kids straining to see who was swinging, and who was missing, and enlisted Red Sox bench coach Mike Stanley to help him with a happy chore.

They rounded up about 10 young fans, found them gloves, Red Sox caps and T-shirts, and invited them to go out on the practice field with the big leaguers and catch fly balls. Always the businessman, Henry made sure the kids' parents signed release forms in case one of their darlings took a Manny Ramirez fly ball off of the coconut, but when those formalities were done, the kids were free to roam the warning track.

None of them caught any fly balls. Red Sox players shagging flies in the outfield saw to that, plus, Pedro Martinez was pitching batting practice, and not many balls even left the infield. Martinez, in many ways a 12-year-old himself, thought the idea was grand. He joked with the kids, autographed everything they stuck in his hands, and said afterwards, "I would see a fly ball going in one direction, and they would be going in the other. I was just hoping nobody got hit on the head."

It was a flabbergasting moment. A year earlier any fan stepping foot on any part of any field would have been chased off as if he or she had scaled the wrought iron fence around 1600 Pennsylvania Avenue. And that's if they were lucky. More likely, any such intruder would have shortly found out what Florida hospitality was like from the inside of the Fort Myers jail.

For years, or for at least as many years as anyone following the Red Sox could remember, the franchise had existed inside of a virtual moat. Being a Red Sox fan was a privilege granted by the team, and for most fans all that the price of a box seat got them was the chance to say "Please sir, may I have another?"

For instance, during the summer of 1999, Bob Hohler began covering the Red Sox for the *Boston Globe* after several years working in that paper's Washington Bureau. Once asked to compare the two beats, Hohler replied, "I've been in the Oval Office, but never in the Red Sox general manager's office."

Under the Harrington administration a couple of fans from Chicago ventured into Boston one winter. They were able to find parking near Fenway and decided to walk around the historic old place, eventually discovering that the main door for deliveries, one near the players' parking lot on Yawkey Way, was open.

They walked up to the security guard at the door and asked him if they might detour under the stands and take a look at the field and Green Monster and bullpens and flagpole and all of the landmarks that made Fenway the most historic standing ballpark in the world.

No, said the guard. And not only could they not step inside the door, if they did not move away from it really, really quickly, he'd call the police and have them arrested for trespassing.

So here, finally, in February in Fort Myers, on the edge of a tangle of brush and swamp land, the prospective new owner of the Red Sox was draining the moat, calling the sharpshooters down from the ramparts, and opening the gates. For the first time since 1933, the "Welcome" sign was up for fans. Things would never be the same, either in Fort Myers, or at the corner of Brookline Avenue and Yawkey Way.

For 70 years, the Boston Red Sox had led the American League in one category—saying "No." When it came to modernizing ancient Fenway Park, the place was too old. When it came to signing African-American players, all of the Sox' farm teams were in the South. When it came to finding players who could run and catch the ball, the Green Monster was too close for that kind of baseball.

That changed on the morning of February 26, 2002, in about the amount of time it takes to play three innings, and it turned out to be the morning that the Red Sox started on their way to winning a World Series.

## It's Official

While Henry's simple gesture on February 26 symbolized the end of the Yawkey years, control of the franchise did not officially change hands until the next day. For most of that day, Henry and Lucchino were in close touch with their financial advisor, David Ginsberg, who was back in Boston signing the reams of paper necessary to close the deal.

While the calendar said it was the end of February, and the map said it was southwest Florida, the weather on February 27 said York Beach, Maine. It was dreadfully cold and windy and the Red Sox' owners-elect spent the bulk of the day inside.

Meanwhile, the players and coaches and managers and general manager went about their business down at the minor-league complex. After their work was done, the public relations staff hosted a cookout for members of the media. This kind of thing was unheard of, of course. During the early part of spring training, when the work was being done at the minor-league fields, reporters were stuffed in a trailer, elbow to elbow, unable to see what was going on out on the fields.

The Red Sox had never provided anything to eat. There was a jug of Florida swamp water in one corner of the trailer, but who knew what microscopic creatures were reproducing in it, so the jug rarely got any use.

The cookout was a revelation, even if the weather was uncooperative. Late in the afternoon, Henry and Lucchino appeared on the scene. They were still waiting to hear from Ginsberg that the deal was done and joined the remaining reporters at the picnic tables outside of the minor-league clubhouse. By now, the hot dogs were cold, but Henry and Lucchino munched away on the leftovers, anyway. No amount of mustard could counter the effects of the chilly wind; after several fruitless calls to Ginsberg, Henry suggested relocating to the main field at the other end of Edison Avenue.

Off he drove with Lucchino, leading a motorcade of reporters, all of them bound to be part of a watershed moment in Red Sox history.

Henry and Lucchino retreated to the relative solitude of John Harrington's old lair, the owners' box down the third-base line, and the wait became baseball's version of electing a pope. How would the new owners signal that the call had come, that the papers had been signed, that the new era had officially begun?

At 5:09 P.M., Lucchino opened the window to the box. He and Henry leaned out and gave a thumbs-up signal. It was done. Sixty-nine years of failure were officially over.

The new owners hollered down that they would be happy to meet with members of the news media on the field. The interviews were done, everyone saying the right things, and the Red Sox' new bosses headed for the right-field grandstand. There, with friends and fellow members of the new management team, they drank cold champagne in the cold citrus breeze.

As the sun set behind the royal palms that encircle the ballpark, Henry and Lucchino finished their drinks, finished their interviews, and strolled slowly down the promenade that separates the box seats from the grandstand at City of Palms Park. Eventually, they turned and disappeared down the tunnel that led from the stadium and into the parking lot.

As they departed, the afternoon had turned to dusk, and though the darkness was about to win out on this day, there was a sense that perhaps new light and new life had finally arrived to rescue the grandest old member of the American League.

## Out with the Old

For two weeks, Dan Duquette had been a man with a title, a paycheck, an office, a secretary, several assistants, and no job to do. He had become a lamer duck than an outgoing Vice-President of the

United States, except that he was the only person in the world of baseball who didn't know it.

Duquette had taken over as general manager of the Red Sox in January of 1994 and when the end came on February 28, 2002, it was hard to imagine that someone who had arrived on the scene with such high hopes had been reduced to playing the role akin to that of a Warsaw Pact dictator, vintage 1989, unaware that the world around him had changed and his palace was about to be ransacked.

New ownership fired Duquette less than 24 hours after formally taking control of the franchise. Henry, Werner and Lucchino had spent the night of February 27 celebrating their takeover. The break-fast menu for their first full day of ownership included scrambling some eggs and frying Duquette. He was gone before the second cup of coffee.

Actually, Duquette was gone long before the official announce-ment. His demise dated back to January, less than a month after Henry's ownership group had reached the agreement to buy the Red Sox from the Yawkey Foundation. Every January, Boston's chapter of the BaseBall Writers Association puts on an awards din-ner. It usually attracts a crowd of one thousand or so fans and they see some Sox players, and some other baseball celebrities, be hon-ored for past performances.

In January of 2002, the dinner was held at the Sheraton-Boston Hotel, its traditional home. That night, Henry rented a suite at the Hilton directly across the street and invited regular baseball beat writers up to visit with him. Each got about 15 minutes with the new owner, and as more than one writer noted, the 15 minutes with the new owner were 15 minutes more than anyone had ever gotten with the old owner.

When the talks, which lasted a couple of hours collectively, were over, Henry was stunned at the depth of the animosity felt by people who covered the team. It had grown beyond dislike to hatred in many instances, and as the new owners talked to more and more people throughout Boston and throughout baseball, they realized how much contempt the Red Sox were held in, and how much of an agent of that contempt Duquette had become.

When spring training finally arrived, Duquette was in Fort Myers as usual but until the ownership papers were signed, he was irrelevant. He occasionally appeared at the workouts and was, of course, asked about his future with the Red Sox. By now, Duquette had become disconnected from the reality of his situation and was Captain Smith on the bridge of the Titanic— Icebergs in the North Atlantic? What are you, crazy?—and told anyone who bothered asking that he had been having discussions with the new owners, had a two-year contract that he looked forward to fulfilling, and that he and Henry's people were on the same page.

In fact, they were not even in the same library.

Duquette was fired first thing on the morning of February 28. The new owners immediately decided to name assistant general manager Mike Port as the interim GM, but had to bypass Sox public relations head Kevin Shea to put together press releases defining the changes. Shea and perhaps farm director Kent Qualls had become the employees most closely aligned with Duquette. Shea in particular had to be kept out of the loop with this news.

There was no immediate response from Duquette after the announcement was made. In the afternoon, however, word came down that he would hold a press conference on the grounds of the luxurious complex he stayed at, the Sanibel Harbor Resort.

He didn't give reporters much lead time, and the resort was several miles from the Red Sox' headquarters in Fort Myers. In late February, that was several miles of traffic lights, stop signs and out-of-state drivers trying to find the Orvis Factory Outlet.

Duquette's firing was the first "Ding-Dong, the Witch is Dead" moment since John McNamara was canned as manager in 1988. Damn the traffic, and at times, damn the red lights—most of the beat reporters who had survived the Duquette years wanted to be there for his farewell press conference.

It was almost pitiful. The staff of the resort had brought out a podium and lined up chairs on either side, ostensibly so Duquette's friends and supporters could be nearby. Out walked Duquette, dressed like Thurston Howell III arriving on Gilligan's Island, and the only friend the ex-general manager had with him was his lawyer, Tony Froio, and Froio's purpose for being on hand seemed to be restricted to glaring at the reporters who had gathered for the farewell. Otherwise, all of those chairs next to the podium were empty.

Duquette had little to say, actually. He was disappointed to not have the chance to bring a World Series winner home to Boston. No one loved the Red Sox more than he did. No one was more dedicated to the team's success. With that, Duquette began to cry. Froio put his arm around his client and walked him back into the complex, towards the swimming pool and into the sorry dungeon of Red Sox history along with the Tom Yawkeys and Joe Cronins and Billy Hermans who had failed before him.

Port's title was Interim General Manager. The last interim anything the Red Sox had appointed was Joe Morgan in 1988, and he lasted 3 ½ memorable seasons. In order to advance from interim to permanent GM, Port's task was essentially what Morgan's was in 1988. Win, and do it dramatically, except that while Morgan had a week, Port had a season.

The new GM was a lifetime baseball man, although he didn't look or act the part. Port had the relaxed, affable demeanor and appearance of a moderately successful Southern California realtor, or perhaps a teaching pro at some Palm Springs country club.

Port also had a very measured, academic way of speaking, as if he had spent a lifetime writing welfare reform legislation. One of his favorite phrases was "due diligence," and he would often drop a "hereunto," a "the aforementioned" or perhaps a "whereas" into conversations. Asked to name his favorite singer, Port might say James

Taylor. Asked to name his favorite James Taylor song, Port might say "Conflagration and Precipitation."

However, Port was one of the few Red Sox front office employees to survive the Duquette years with his reputation intact. Although he was often used by Duquette to deliver bad news, Port was viewed as honest, decent, responsible and fair-minded.

In other words, exactly what the new ownership needed to help the Red Sox restore their standing in the baseball community, and in the end, he would turn out to be the Gerald Ford of the grand old franchise.

Unlike Duquette, Port had actually played professional baseball. He was a Southern California kid, a second baseman of apparently limited ability. He broke into the minors with the Padres organization just as they entered the National League and one day in 1969 was told that the organization had found the perfect spot for his talents.

They released him as a player and made him general manager of their farm team in Key West, Florida where he worked with Don Zimmer some years before Zimmer arrived in Boston. Port made his way up through the Padres organization, then joined the California Angels. In September of 1984, he was named interim GM of the Angels, replacing Buzzie Bavasi.

"When I took over in Anaheim," Port said after he was announced as Duquette's replacement, "I was the interim GM there, too. That lasted, I guess, six or seven years."

During those six or seven years, Port worked for Gene Autry. He played host to Richard Nixon, a big Angels fan, and got to know Autry's pal Pat Buttram, best known as Mr. Haney from Green Acres. He saw Telly Savalas at the Angels games and Richard Farnsworth and found time to put together a team that won the AL West title in 1986.

The Autry entourage was an endless source of stories, as were Port's days in Key West, which by 1969 was well on its way to becoming Margaritaville.

His best baseball stories included one about Jimmy Allen, a left-handed pitcher who was afflicted with lazy eye. Far from being a handicap, that ailment allowed Allen to look at home plate and first base at the same time, making him almost impossible to steal on. Port also enjoyed telling how Hollywood producer Aaron Spelling had gone to a game in El Paso, Texas, where the Angels had their Double A minor league affiliate. At the time, El Paso was managed by Lawrence "Moose" Stubing, who also managed the Angels very briefly. Spelling liked Stubing so much that when he put together a new TV show about a Pacific cruise ship, he named the captain after the El Paso manager, which is how Captain Merrill Stubing came to command "The Love Boat."

When the last day of the first February of John Henry's ownership of the Red Sox was over, the franchise was finally turned in a direction that would lead it to a World Championship, and sooner rather than later, although no one knew it at the time. Harrington was gone, and with him all of the baggage of the Yawkey decades. Now, Duquette was gone and it was as though a general amnesty had been declared for all of those Red Sox employees who had dared to think original thoughts, but had been discouraged from ever acting on them.

The major moves had been made, and it had been easy. There was still some tidying up to do, though, and the next item on the agenda was the manager.

## The Grady Bunch

Joe Kerrigan had shown up for spring training knowing that his future as manager was tenuous. He had done a lousy job finishing the 2001 season, for one. Then the ownership that paid him, and the general manager who hired him, were both gone by the beginning of March.

He quickly became Dead Man Managing.

Even so, Kerrigan conducted himself professionally. He was asked about his future on a daily basis and repeated the same answer on a daily basis—he and the new management had talked, the talk was upbeat and pleasant, but he had no idea what would happen. "I know," Kerrigan said, "that you guys think I stay up until 3:30 in the morning every day worrying about my job, but that's just not the case."

Kerrigan went to bed one final time as Sox manager on March 4. He was fired after an exhibition game on Tuesday, March 5, and came to City of Palms Park the next day to meet with reporters.

His press conference was informal. It was held in the open-air concourse outside of the Red Sox clubhouse and Kerrigan was composed as he talked about his disappointment at being fired, and about how he actually had known for days that the new owners would not bring him back. Suddenly, he broke down in tears, turned, and walked away. It was his last act as manager.

The former pitching coach departed having had the shortest tenure of any permanent Red Sox manager since 1906, when Chick Stahl killed himself during spring training and the team went through four managers in the aftermath.

Kerrigan was immediately replaced by third base coach Mike Cubbage, although it was made clear that Cubbage would only handle the team until a permanent successor could be found. Cubbage was on the list of candidates, but told friends who called him with congratulations that he really didn't think he would be hired full-time.

As usual, the name of Felipe Alou came up on that list of candidates, along with Ken Macha, Tony Pena and Grady Little, who had been Jimy Williams' bench coach from 1997 through 1999. Little was immensely popular with Sox players who had been on the team in those years, but it was easy for coaches to be immensely popular since they never had to make any decisions about who would be in the lineup and who would not.

The Sox had announced that Cubbage was a candidate and would be interviewed. Beyond that, they tried to keep things secret, but these new owners were not cut out to be spies. They brought Little in to City of Palms Park for an interview, but when he headed downstairs from the executive offices, he walked into an elevator full of reporters.

Three days later, those same reporters were standing outside of the Sox clubhouse waiting for news on the naming of a new manager, when they heard loud applause from behind the door. When it opened, Little was inside, having been introduced as Kerrigan's replacement.

Little had been a catcher in the minor leagues. When his playing career ended, he tried cotton farming near Abilene, Texas. Had it been 1945 and not 1975, Little might have made a living from the land, but by the time he went into business, the day of the family farm was running out of sunlight. By the beginning of the 1980s, Little was back in baseball as a minor-league manager.

He was a very good one and had some tremendous teams in the Braves' farm system. Little finally landed in the majors as a bullpen coach with the Padres, then came to Boston when Williams was hired. Little had relocated to Pinehurst, North Carolina by the time the Sox hired him and he had more than a little Andy Griffith in him. Little spoke with a soft southern accent that was almost a monotone, and had an equally understated sense of humor. He had managed a bit in the majors as a fill-in when Williams got suspended, and then went to Cleveland where he substituted for Indians manager Charlie Manuel after Manuel fell ill.

Asked once why he thought he'd make a good big-league manager, Little responded, "People know that I've been associated with winning a lot," which was the kind of comment almost guaranteed to come back to haunt whoever said it.

At the time the Sox hired Little, the start of the regular season was less than a month away. They needed someone who knew a little about the organization, and about the talent, someone who could make the transition from Kerrigan as seamless as possible.

The transition was smooth enough, but not seamless, as the Sox would find out in the autumn of 2004. But with both Duquette and Kerrigan gone, and Port and Little hired—at least for a year—the old guard was officially gone, and the Red Sox' version of the New Deal had begun in earnest.

# SNAPSHOT

## The Oldest Red Sox

Only one Red Sox player has lived to be 100 years old.

Milt Gaston was born in Ridgefield Park, New Jersey on January 27, 1896 and died in Marston's Mills, Massachusetts on April 26, 1996. Eleven of Gaston's 100 years were spent as a major league pitcher, three of those with the Red Sox.

In the spring of 1992 Gaston was 96 and living in a condominium in Bradenton, Florida, just a couple of blocks from where the Pirates held spring training at McKechnie Field. On March 27 of that year, the Red Sox were playing Pittsburgh in Bradenton, so a couple of days ahead of time I checked directory assistance to see if there was a listing for a Milt Gaston in that city. There was, I dialed the number, and he answered. Sure, he said, come on up any time. He'd be glad to talk.

And Gaston did talk that day, for most of the morning. At 96, he was a widower, but he lived by himself with occasional visits from a neighbor who checked in on him and helped him with the housekeeping. His memory was stunningly focused and talking with him was about as close to time travel as anyone could get.

Gaston pitched in the majors from 1924 through 1934. He was in Boston from 1929 to 1931 and his career record of 27-52 is one of the worst by any Red Sox starter. He had only one memorable season, his first, in 1924 when he was with the Yankees and played with Babe Ruth and Lou Gehrig.

The Sox got him in a trade with the Washington Senators and in those dreadful years, he was one of their most reliable pitchers. Gaston might have lasted longer with Boston had he not hurt his arm in 1931.

"In those days," he remembered, "nobody knew what was wrong with your arm. Now, you hear talk about the rotator cuff. Well, they'd never heard of that thing back then, but I think that's probably what was wrong with me.

"Anyway, the team sent me to see this arm specialist in Indianapolis, Doc Ferguson, and when I got there I went to his office. He had this human arm hanging in a tub of formaldehyde, and he'd manipulate the tendons and the fingers would move, and I wasn't in there too long before I told him, 'Please, Doc. No more. I've seen enough.' And it all came down to the fact that he couldn't help me, so I went back to Boston."

There were no guaranteed contracts back then. If you didn't play, you didn't get paid, so the bad teams in the major leagues were loaded with guys who were hurt but would not admit it. Gaston was one of them.

"After that," he said, "Every time I threw it hurt like hell, but I didn't tell anyone. Couldn't, because they would have gotten rid of me. So, for the last three years I bluffed my way through."

Gaston played in a Fenway Park that was mostly empty, but enjoyed his time in town. Back then, city bylaws didn't allow for baseball games near churches on Sunday. There was a church near Fenway, so the Sox played their Sunday games at Braves Field. Gaston remembered that he once beat the White Sox at Braves Field in a game that lasted 69 minutes. And he was right. It was the first game of a doubleheader on August 24, 1930 and Boston won it, 2-0.

His biggest salary with the Sox was $10,000, a ton of money during the Great Depression. How he broke into baseball is a classic example of how uncomplicated the game was back then—Gaston was working in City Hall in New York and pitching in a semi-pro league in Paterson, New Jersey on weekends. The Yanks heard about him, scouted him, and then signed him for a $5,000 bonus. Gaston is one of the few major leaguers who never spent a day in the minors.

He roomed with Gehrig on the Yankees and once made the mistake of agreeing to a friendly wrestling match with him. Gehrig, a gentle man, nearly broke Gaston in half and that was the end of the wrestling, friendly or not.

While with the Sox, Gaston was pals with pitcher Ed Morris, a tragic figure who died in March of 1932 after being stabbed at a cookout in Florida by a jealous husband. By then, Gaston was with the White Sox, but through friends he heard the story of what happened. While the cause of Morris' death has always been listed as knife wounds, Gaston believed that it was actually hypothermia. After being stabbed, a crazed Morris dove into a nearby lake and swam to the opposite shore. Cold and drained by the loss of blood, Morris died.

The ugly incident was not entirely out of character, Gaston said. He remembered being at a hotel in Detroit with Morris and his teammate had gotten drunk at the bar. Gaston left for his room just ahead of Morris and hopped an elevator, with Morris opting for the next one going up. Morris and a man he had been talking with at the bar got on the elevator together. By the time it had stopped at the floor the Sox were staying on, Morris had beaten the other hotel guest into a bloody mess.

After his career ended, Gaston settled in Florida and did a number of things. He eventually became a sergeant in the Tampa sheriff's department and worked there until he retired. Through the years he would get old baseballs and cards and odd souvenirs in the mail and would patiently sign every item and send it back.

"I never refuse to sign things," he said. "That's the thing I don't understand, these fellas getting paid for everything they sign. I don't go for that. They're making plenty of money. Another thing—if they wanted to take the millions that these guys make and slice a little off, they could take care of all the old-timers."

Shortly before I spent the morning with Milt Gaston, he had been interviewed by Ken Burns for Burns' PBS documentary on baseball. "It's supposed to be on TV in 1994," Gaston said. "I hope I'm here to see it, but I doubt it."

Gaston made it. As his health began to slip, he moved to Cape Cod to be with relatives. He was one day shy of being 100 years, four months old when he passed away in Marston's Mills, the only man to play for the Red Sox who ever made it to the century mark.

# A Brief Look Back
## 1901 through 1986

THE RED SOX, AS IT TURNED OUT, DIDN'T EVEN HAVE TO MAKE A down payment to own the hearts of Boston's baseball fans.

Boston was the kettle in which the emotions that led to the American Revolution were brewed, so it is little wonder that baseball's great revolution of 1901 was so well-received there.

By the beginning of the 20th Century, major league baseball had grown stale. The National League had established a dreary monopoly and nowhere were fans more bored than in Boston. Their National League team had been one of the best in the league since it began play in 1876, but penurious ownership and a non-descript little ballpark had sapped fans' enthusiasm.

In 1901, Ban Johnson decided to take his Western League to the next level and make it a major league, in direct competition with the staid old NL. The new American League was very much a closed corporation. Johnson ran it and had financial backing from Cleveland's Charles Somers, who invested in several franchises including the one in Boston. When it came time to sign a lease for a ballpark in Boston, it was done by Connie Mack, acting as an agent for the American League. Mack owned a chunk of the Philadelphia team as well as managed it.

Boston's National League team, which had come to be known as the Beaneaters, was essentially run by Arthur Soden, an old-style businessman who could squeeze the copper out of a penny. Soden's legacy was the Reserve Clause, the fine print on a baseball contract that bound a player to his team for life, at least in the National League. A Soden invention, the Reserve Clause kept salaries artificially low until the 1970s, when arbitrator Peter Seitz finally ruled it illegal.

Until 1894, the Beaneaters played in a lovely, double-decked ballpark in Boston's South End. During the 1894 season, the park burned down. Soden had underinsured it, so he replaced it with a utilitarian, scaled-down version where the team played until 1914, when it moved to Fenway Park during the Miracle Braves run.

When the American League came to town in 1901, the new team—initially called the Americans—immediately grabbed four of Soden's best players by the time-honored tactic of offering more money. Pitcher Ted Lewis, premier third baseman Jimmy Collins, center fielder Chick Stahl and first baseman Buck Freeman jumped to the Boston Americans as did pitcher Nig Cuppy, whose career was winding down. In 1902, after Lewis left baseball to pursue a career in academia, pitcher Bill Dinneen came over from the Beaneaters and the raid was complete. The new franchise's signature player, pitcher Cy Young, was snatched from St. Louis before the 1901 season.

The new team set up shop in 1901 off of Huntington Avenue, just across the railroad tracks from the Beaneaters' field on Walpole Street. One of the most stunning photographs of the era, taken from a distance, shows fans swarming onto the Huntington Avenue Grounds diamond during the 1903 World Series. In the background, beyond the smoke of the locomotives, stands the Beaneaters' little park, empty and forlorn.

Boston's baseball fans deserted the Beaneaters as fast as the players did. The National League team had drawn 202,000 fans in 1900. That dropped to 146,500 in 1901 after the Americans started play and was just 116,960 by 1902. In contrast, the Americans drew

289,448 in 1901 and 379,338 in 1902. They had, in baseball terms, captured the city overnight.

And, in fact, they really never relinquished control. The 1920s were a disastrous decade for the Sox, but the National League team—the Braves by then—was equally bad. Even in 1948, when the Sox finished second in a playoff and the Braves won the National League pennant, the Red Sox' attendance was larger.

While Sox fans of the second half of the 20th Century always figured that their team's timing was terrible, it was actually perfect during the franchise's early years. After grabbing away the Beaneaters' best players and their fans, in 1901 and 1902, the Americans won the pennant in 1903 and 1904. The 1903 pennant was followed by the first World Series, won by Boston, and as difficult as it might be to believe when looking at pictures of the stone-faced, top-hatted folks from the early 1900s, they were as maniacally attached to the team as the people who paid $85 for box seats, and $30 to park, in 2005.

In 1909, with a third place team that finished 9 ½ games out of first place, the Red Sox drew 668,965 to the primitive wooden ballpark on Huntington Avenue, an attendance figure that would not be bettered until the post-war euphoria of 1946.

The Huntington Avenue era ended in 1911, the final season before Fenway Park opened. Up until that time, the pennants in 1903 and 1904 were the only ones won by the Red Sox—who began being called that in 1907—and they were followed quickly by the disaster of 1906, when the team lost 20 games in a row at one point and finished 49-105. The franchise was able to rebuild in short order, though. In 1907 it brought up teenaged rookie Tris Speaker from the minors; he became a regular in 1909. The Sox signed third baseman Larry Gardner out of the University of Vermont in 1908, and signed 19-year-old pitcher Smoky Joe Wood, who could have joined his friend Speaker in the Hall of Fame had he not been hurt after the 1912 season.

In 1909, the Red Sox added outfielder Harry Hooper—another Hall of Famer—and dependable second baseman Steve Yerkes.

Duffy Lewis came aboard in 1910, and most of the pieces were in place for the greatest decade in Boston baseball history.

In 1912, the team left Huntington Avenue for a new home, Fenway Park, and had a new manager in Jake Stahl. The result was the most successful season in franchise history and the dawn of the golden age of major league baseball in Boston.

From 1912 through 1918, the Red Sox won four World Series in a span of seven seasons. In one of those seasons, 1914, the downtrodden Braves won the National League pennant, coming from last place in July to do it. It is a season that is comparable to 1967 for the Red Sox, or 1969 for the Mets, and perhaps even more remarkable, but has faded in memory and awaits for some baseball archeologist to bring it back to life.

The five World Championships in seven seasons for the same city is surpassed only by New York's dominance of the baseball world when the Yankees, Giants and Dodgers combined to win the World Series 10 times in 12 years from 1947 to 1958.

The 1912 to 1918 Red Sox were dynastic in their results, but hardly monolithic. The franchise had four different owners—John I. Taylor, James McAleer, Joe Lannin and Harry Frazee—and four different managers. Stahl was fired halfway through the 1913 season and replaced by catcher Bill Carrigan, and he went home to become a banker in Lewiston, Maine after the 1916 title. Jack Barry managed in 1917, then left for World War I and was replaced by Ed Barrow. Outfielder Harry Hooper was the only player to participate in all four of the Sox' World Series wins.

Speaker was traded to Cleveland after the 1915 season because of contract issues. As one future Hall of Famer left, another arrived in the person of Babe Ruth, who first came up as a teenager late in the 1914 season.

On occasion, someone in the baseball world will open the ridiculous debate of who is the greatest player of all-time. It is not an arguable point, and the answer is Ruth. Ruth was at first one of the greatest pitchers of his era, then later became its greatest hitter. That just about covers the possibilities. Imagine if Bobby Orr had been one of the best skaters and also one of the best goalies in hockey. Or if Jimmy Brown had been as good at linebacker as he was at running back for the NFL's Cleveland Browns.

Ruth helped pitch the Red Sox to championships in 1915 and 1916, and looking back, the 1916 team really marked the end of the dynasty. Boston won the pennant, and World Series, again in 1918, but that was a different club entirely. World War I had siphoned off many of the game's best players, and the 16 major league teams essentially had to become Cadillacs assembled from parts picked up at the junkyard. The Red Sox happened to be the best jalopy.

And they began to break down in 1919, the first year of Boston's hideous journey into baseball infamy. By then, the Braves had long since reverted to form and were annually buried near the bottom of the National League. In 1919, the Red Sox dropped below .500 for the first time since 1908. Over the course of the next 33 baseball seasons, with two teams in town, Boston celebrated exactly two pennants, one by the Red Sox in 1946, and another by the Braves in 1948.

From 1919 through 1933, Boston's major league baseball teams lost almost 1,000 more games than they won—1,835-2,730; combined to finish last 12 times, lost 100 or more games nine times, and had two seasons above .500, both by the Braves.

The abdication of the Red Sox as emperors of baseball had begun even before Frazee sold Babe Ruth on December 26, 1919, but it gained unstoppable momentum after that.

The true story about the sale of Ruth and the subsequent disintegration of the Red Sox franchise has been aptly told in Glenn Stout and Dick Johnson's landmark work *Red Sox Century*. The sale of Ruth was a mistake, but not part of some sinister plot to destroy the Sox for the sake of the Yankees.

That is what the effect was, however, and it took four score and six years for Boston to repeat the World Championship of 1918.

The seasons from 1919 through 1933 were a series of relentless, unmitigated disasters for the Red Sox and their shrinking fan base. Frazee finally sold out on August 1, 1923 to a group headed by baseball insider Bob Quinn. Quinn, however, had no money of his own. The man with the cash was a Midwestern businessman, Palmer Winslow. But within three years, Winslow was dead. Quinn had no farm system, no money, a deteriorating ballpark and played in a two-team city with barely enough fans to go around for one.

It bottomed out in 1932, when the Sox went 43-111 and averaged fewer than 2,400 customers a game. Quinn finally sold out to Thomas A. Yawkey, a rich young man who had lots of money, not a penny of which he had earned through hard work.

In light of what the Red Sox quickly became under Yawkey, a collection of plodding home run hitters, it is interesting to hear what he had to say to baseball writer Bill Cunningham in a 1933 article in *Collier's* magazine:

"But who bothers with any real base stealing today? Somebody tries it occasionally, but what's the use with every batter coming up to take a free swing, a swing that likely as not will slam the ball into the center field clock?

"My idea of baseball is to outthink the other fellow, outguess him, run him crazy by crossing him up. I want another Wee Willie Keeler who can hit 'em where they ain't. I want a club that won't depend upon brute strength alone."

Within five years of when he purchased the Red Sox, Yawkey's roster was the ultimate in brute strength baseball, and occasionally just plain brutal baseball.

Yawkey bought a team that played in a ballpark that, 20 years after it opened, was decrepit and obsolete. His farm system consisted of two Class B teams. The 1932 team employed 41 different players, 15 of whom never appeared in a major league game again.

Yawkey proceeded to go out and buy himself a contender, throwing his hard-inherited money at the other have-not teams in the

American League like Washington and the Philadelphia A's, owned by Mack, who had never recovered from the stock market crash of 1929.

Yawkey rebuilt Fenway Park before the 1934 season, and its essentials remained the same 70 years later. Also in 1934 he acquired Lefty Grove and Wes Ferrell; in 1935 he got Joe Cronin; and before the 1936 season began, he got Jimmie Foxx. By 1937, he had expanded the farm system from those two measly teams to 11.

But, he never bought, or developed, enough pitching to compete with the Yankees.

For all of his attention to improving the Red Sox, Yawkey never really even came close to winning a pennant until 1946. In all of those prior years, 1933 to 1945, no Boston team was ever within five games of first place on September 1.

If World War II had not come along, perhaps the Red Sox would have caught up to the Yankees sooner. After his initial orgy of spending on established stars, Yawkey got more patient. He signed future Hall of Famers Ted Williams and Bobby Doerr out of the Pacific Coast League and started developing players like shortstop Johnny Pesky from a farm system supervised by ex-umpire Billy Evans. Perhaps it all would have jelled by 1943 or 1944 if the war had not intervened; however, in 1946 the pieces all came together for the Sox' first pennant since 1918 and their best record since 1912.

Boston played the Cardinals in the World Series and lost in seven games, the franchise's first-ever Series defeat. But, it did not seem to be the end of the world. The Sox were in their collective primes; there would be more pennants forthcoming. And, in fact, after stumbling in 1947, Boston essentially tied for first in 1948 and 1949.

But lost both playoff games. In 1948, the Red Sox lost to the Indians at Fenway Park in an official playoff game when manager Joe McCarthy decided to use Denny Galehouse to start. In 1949, the playoff was unofficial, but the season came down to one final game at Yankee Stadium and New York won it.

Boston contended again in both 1950 and 1951. In 1950, McCarthy quit as manager in June and was replaced by Steve O'Neill, who had caught for Boston during the dark days of the Quinn era in 1924. Under O'Neill, the Sox closed fast and on the morning of September 20, were 89-53, a half-game behind the Yankees at 90-53. New York, of course, prevailed. In 1951, Boston was as close to the Yanks as 2 ½ games on September 17, but folded badly down the stretch.

The next time Boston would be in a pennant race in September was 1967.

In the meantime, the franchise fell back on hard times. They were not hard times like the Quinn years, not desperate and depressing. The Red Sox became an uninteresting team run by a disinterested owner in the increasingly absent Yawkey. Lou Boudreau, who beat the Sox in the 1948 playoff while player-manager at Cleveland, took over for O'Neill and undertook a youth movement that dismantled what was left of the post-War powerhouse, save for Williams.

For most of the Yawkey ownership, the franchise's racism was of no consequence since the entire sorry lot of baseball's lords were content to maintain the color line. But when it fell in 1946 with the Dodgers' signing of Jackie Robinson, the Red Sox began falling behind. By 1952, it had begun to have an effect on their fortunes. Still, Yawkey might have been forced to integrate if the Braves had not moved to Milwaukee after the 1952 season.

While the Braves had never provided much competition for the affections, and dollars, of Boston's baseball fans, they were on the verge of becoming one of the game's best teams when they left for Wisconsin, and they did it because they had been quick to tap into the new talent pool provided by integration. When the Braves won the National League pennant in Milwaukee in 1957, they had five key players—Hank Aaron, Billy Bruton, Wes Covington, Felix Mantilla and Juan Pizarro—whom the Red Sox would never have employed.

There is no proving it, but it seems reasonable to figure that in the face of competition from the great Braves teams of the mid to late

1950s, Yawkey's Red Sox would have been forced to follow suit to hold onto their fans. Instead, they let the interest generated by Williams carry them along on a wave of mediocrity. As Williams stayed, his old friends from the great years left. Pesky was traded. Doerr retired, as did Dom DiMaggio when Boudreau decided he had gotten too old. The Red Sox decided they had had enough of Boudreau after a terrible year in 1954 when they went 69-85.

He was replaced by Mike Higgins, a former Sox third baseman who had once gotten base hits in 12 consecutive at bats. Higgins had played for Boston's 1946 pennant winner, then gone into managing. He had moved up the ladder quickly and his teams had excellent records. Every stop Higgins had made, though, was in the south. First, Roanoke, Virginia in the Piedmont League. Then on to Birmingham, Alabama. And finally four years in Louisville.

A native of Texas, Higgins was one of the many bigots in the big leagues and he would be one of the last to be overtly so. The mystery is how Higgins lasted as long as he did. He managed the Red Sox from 1955 into the 1959 season, when he was fired halfway through and replaced by Billy Jurges. Jurges was then canned midway through the 1960 season and replaced by Higgins. He then managed through 1962.

In all that time, the Red Sox never once contended. Still, Higgins is second only to Joe Cronin in longevity among Boston's managers. He was Yawkey's own Rasputin. Higgins wasn't even fired as manager. He was promoted to General Manager, where he was a failure in 1963 and 1964 with Pesky as manager, then again in 1965 with Billy Herman.

Higgins was part of a general malaise around the franchise. Malaise, bigotry and alcohol—they were a deadly formula for failure. After Cronin took over as president of the American League, Yawkey brought in Bucky Harris as GM, and Harris was old and tired by then, not up to the job. Harris was a drinker, too. Dick O'Connell, the business manager then and later general manager, once said that one of his chores under Harris was to help the old man sign papers because his hands shook so badly.

In 1959, a year after the NHL Bruins employed black winger Willie O'Ree, the Red Sox finally used a black player, infielder Pumpsie Green. Green was a good utility player, nothing more, and one of the most admirable things about Ted Williams was how graciously he treated Green after he arrived in Boston.

Not that everyone treated Green the way that Williams did. In an interview for Steve Buckley's book *Red Sox: Where Have You Gone?* Green relates that one night Sox coach Del Baker was in the dugout and using vile words to describe Indians outfielder Minnie Minoso, a Cuban, with Green within earshot.

Green was dumbfounded and wondered how to react. Before he had to, pitcher Bill Monbouquette went over and told Baker, "Del— Pumpsie's here now. You can't talk that way any more."

Williams retired after the 1960 season and attendance dropped by about 275,000. In 1961, Carl Yastrzemski debuted, in 1962 Dick Radatz, in 1963 Dave Morehead and Rico Petrocelli, and in 1964 Tony Conigliaro. Despite the infusion of young talent—all of it still white—Boston remained a non-factor in the pennant race every year.

The hiring of the popular Pesky in 1963 did give the team a boost and he had the Sox in contention into July, after which they faded badly. With Higgins providing no help at all as GM, Pesky was fired after the 1964 season and replaced by third base coach Billy Herman, a member of baseball's old guard and a manager built for comfort, not speed.

By the time Herman was hired, it had been more than 10 years since the Red Sox had fielded a contender. Interest in the team was as low as it had been since the Bob Quinn days. In his song, "Stones," Neil Diamond sings that "Being lost is worth the coming home;" perhaps he had the Impossible Dream in mind at the time.

How much less memorable would the Impossible Dream have been had not the Sox been so bad for so long? Were those long seasons of denial worth it for the increased joy of what happened in 1967? They are unanswerable questions, but for sure, Sox fans who had endured all of the bad years knew how Jed Clampett felt when up from the ground came a bubbling crude. The Impossible Dream made them rich beyond their wildest fantasies.

Defining the timeline of the Impossible Dream is easy, at least in retrospect. It began on September 16, 1965 when Higgins was finally fired as general manager while Morehead was pitching a no-hitter against Cleveland in a deserted Fenway Park. This time, there was no bringing Higgins back in any capacity. His time with the Red Sox was through, and digging the franchise out from under the debris he left behind was surprisingly easy.

Yawkey hired O'Connell as the new GM. O'Connell had never gotten 12 straight hits, had never played in a World Series and had no drinking buddies from his playing days to reward. O'Connell was not a ballplayer at all. He was an executive and came to the job with no baggage or preconceived notions or, most importantly, racial prejudices.

He inherited Herman as his manager and kept him for the 1966 season. The 1965 Sox had been the first Boston team to lose 100 games since 1932. The 1966 Sox finished just a half-game out of 10th place. Herman has gone down in history as a do-nothing manager, the Warren G. Harding of the Boston dugout, but he perhaps deserves a bit more credit than that.

In 1966, the Sox debuted George Scott at first base, Scott becoming Boston's first-ever black position player signed by Sox scouts and developed in the farm system. Joe Foy, also black, was the third baseman. George Smith, a former member of the all-black Indianapolis Clowns, played second. O'Connell had wasted little time making his presence known.

On July 4, Herman's Sox were 28-51. After that, they went 44-39, a winning percentage of .530. It was the prelude to the Impossible Dream, but Herman never gets much credit for it, since he wasn't around for it. He was fired with 16 games left in the year and replaced on an interim basis by Pete Runnels.

O'Connell hired Dick Williams as the permanent manager for 1967 and the Red Sox produced what can be argued is the most dramatic, compelling and memorable single season in baseball history. Perhaps the 1914 Miracle Braves are comparable, or the 1969 Mets, but probably not. Imagine the 2004 Red Sox post-season, but on a weekly basis for three months. That was the second half of the Impossible Dream, and that the Sox lost the World Series to the Cardinals was irrelevant at the time.

The World Champion Red Sox of 2004 were direct descendants of the Impossible Dream Sox. The 1967 season created a Sox hysteria that occasionally waned, but never went away. For those who experienced it, the Impossible Dream remains the most profound and enduring memory of their lives as baseball fans.

Before 2004, fans would occasionally approach me to talk about the Red Sox' long list of tantalizing failures. If they were old enough to remember 1967, I would ask them, "Given the chance by a higher power who offered you a deal, would you take the Sox finishing second in 1967 in exchange for them winning the World Series in 1986?"

About 80 percent of the time, fans chose winning in 1967.

The Impossible Dream was a tangible, visible, easily recognized boundary between the old Yawkey Sox and the new ones. While from 1952 to 1966, Boston teams never contended, and from 1959 through 1966, never broke the .500 mark, in 1967 they started a streak of playing better than .500 baseball for 16 consecutive seasons. From 1967 through 2001, the final year of the Yawkey Dynasty, the Red Sox played above .500 in 29 of 36 seasons; finished first six times; and were in the pennant race in September 14 times.

While Boston came close to finishing first in both 1972 and 1974—both times reviving memories of the awful late-season defeats in 1948 and 1949—it finally got back into the World Series in 1975, losing in seven games to the Reds in what remains one of the great events in the history of the game. That 1975 team was the culmination of years of effort put into player development by O'Connell and his staff. Eight of the nine regulars in the batting order were home-grown, and from 1975 through the arrival of Dan Duquette in 1994, Boston remained a franchise built around a productive farm system.

The seeds for the 1975 pennant were actually sown amidst the rubble of the 1974 fold. On August 21 and August 23 of 1974, Rogelio Moret and Luis Tiant pitched back to back shutouts that moved the Red Sox into a seven-game lead in the AL East title race. After that, Boston proceeded to lose 11 of its next 13 games, and all seven games of that lead. By the end of the season, the Sox were seven games out of first place, a negative swing of 14 games in a span of 38.

The collapse happened because the team collectively stopped hitting, but help arrived in the middle of the slump, although no one knew at the time just how much help it would turn out to be. On August 19, rookie Jim Rice—called up from Pawtucket where he was Minor League Player of the Year—made his major league debut and on September 5, after the Pawtucket season ended, rookie Fred Lynn broke into the big leagues.

Rice batted .269 and hit his first home run on the next to last day of the season in a meaningless 7-4 victory over the Indians. Lynn was more impressive. He hit .419 in 15 games and added two home runs. Neither played enough to use up his rookie eligibility. Both were Rookie of the Year candidates in the Red Sox' pennant run in 1975. Lynn won the award, along with Most Valuable Player, and the Sox cruised into the post season where they swept the Athletics in the ALCS, then took on Cincinnati in the World Series.

If not the greatest World Series ever played, it was one of the greatest. By any definition, it was the most memorable set of games any Red Sox team has ever played. The teams went back and forth through the first five games with the favored Reds taking a 3 games to 2 lead into Fenway Park for the final two games.

Game 6 ranks with Bobby Thomson's "The Giants Win the Pennant" game as the greatest in the history of baseball. Almost hopelessly behind, the Red Sox tied it 6-6 in the eighth inning on Bernie Carbo's three-run homer, a home run that came one pitch after what looked like a hopeless swing. Carlton Fisk won it in the last of the 12th with a game-ending solo homer off of the left-field foul pole.

Boston took an early 3-0 lead in Game 7, but Cincinnati won it, and the series, 4-3. It was a season, and a World Series, that re-invigorated a franchise that had started to run out of the adrenaline created by the Impossible Dream, and with Rice and Lynn and Fisk, and Rick Burleson and Dwight Evans, just approaching their primes, it seemed inevitable that Boston would have many more chances to be world champions.

But it did not happen.

The Sox almost won again in 1977 and 1978, with the second-half fold and subsequent playoff loss to the Yankees ranking at the top of the long list of disappointments for Boston's baseball fans. The 1978 loss soured fans on manager Don Zimmer, who should have been fired for his own sake after that, much as Grady Little would be 25 years later.

Yawkey had died midway through 1976. With his death control of the franchise passed to his widow, Jean. She retained control of things—sometimes from up close, sometimes from a distance—until she died after the 1991 season. But on the field, little changed. The Red Sox always entertained, often contended, occasionally finished first and never won the World Series.

They did not even return to the World Series until 1986. Boston won the AL East easily, then beat the Angels in the ALCS in a remarkable comeback fueled by Dave Henderson's one-strike-away home run in Game 5. A few days later, the Sox would be one-strike-away themselves, this time in a Game 6, this time in the World Series, and the result was only too predictable, even if it was not too unexpected.

Boston played the Mets in the World Series and won the first two games, both in New York. Winning the first two games of the World Series on the road was not a guarantee of ultimate victory, but was close to it. The Mets turned things around as soon as they reached Fenway Park, as Lenny Dykstra led off Game 3 with a home run into the seats near Pesky's Pole.

New York won both the third and fourth games at Fenway to tie the series at 2-2, but Bruce Hurst prevailed in Game 5 and the teams returned to New York with the Red Sox just one victory away.

The game was tied at 3-3 going into the top of the 10th. The amazing Henderson homered to make it 4-3, then Boston added another run and was up by two with three outs left to get.

In the last of the 10th, with Calvin Schiraldi pitching for the Red Sox, Wally Backman flied to left and Keith Hernandez to center. The Mets had two out and nobody on base. Four batters later, they had won.

Gary Carter, pinch-hitter Kevin Mitchell and then Ray Knight all singled off of Schiraldi to make it 5-4 and put Mets at first and third. Bob Stanley relieved Schiraldi to face Mookie Wilson and got two strikes on Wilson, then threw a ball to the backstop that allowed Mitchell to score and Knight to move to second.

Wilson then hit a slow grounder to first that went through Bill Buckner's legs and into shallow right field. Knight scored the winning run and while the series was officially tied, it was unofficially over. The Mets won Game 7 and were world champions.

While Buckner has been blamed for the Game 6 loss, and manager John McNamara indirectly blamed for leaving the limp-legged first baseman in the game, it was lost with Stanley's wild pitch. Just as the Angels had previously lost the ALCS when Henderson tied Game 5 with his ninth inning homer. The crater created by the kind of emotional impact is hard to overcome. Buckner was merely the handiest, and most easily identifiable, target.

The immediate impact of Boston's World Series defeat was to

plunge New England into a collective sense of despair that lasted through a dreary autumn and cheerless winter. The sun eventually came out again, at least for the tomato plants and forsythias and robins, but the good people of the region would have to walk around with what seemed like an eternal knot in their tummies.

That eternity lasted for 18 years.

# SNAPSHOT

## The Greatest Comeback Ever

The ultimate appeal of baseball may be the game's complete disdain for logic.

Dave Morehead and Matt Young both pitched no-hitters for the Red Sox. Roger Clemens never did. The last triple Rich Gedman ever hit in the major leagues was on September 18, 1985, a night in which he also singled, doubled and homered to hit for the cycle.

Which explains why a real lousy Red Sox team authored the greatest comeback in franchise history on Father's Day 1961.

Boston played the expansion Washington Senators in a doubleheader on that day and, with two out in the bottom of the ninth of the first game, was down by a score of 12-5. That's right—down by seven runs with one out to go, as hopeless as Barry Goldwater on the eve of the 1964 presidential election.

The Red Sox won, 13-12.

I remember watching the game on TV and 30 years later decided to try to track down some of the key participants and see if they remembered it which, of course, they did.

Boston scored three runs on a single by Carroll Hardy and two bases-loaded walks before catcher Jim Pagliaroni hit a grand slam into the screen to make it 12-12. After that, Vic Wertz walked, Don Buddin singled, and Russ Nixon singled home the winning run.

13-12.

The losing pitcher was Dave Sisler, a tall, scholarly Princeton alum who had once pitched for the Red Sox, and whose family tree included Hall of Fame talent.

"It was the lowlight of my career," he said when I called him in St. Louis, where he had become a prosperous stockbroker. "I remember that it was so bad that, between games of the doubleheader, two little girls sent me a note in the clubhouse saying how bad they felt for me."

Sisler was on in relief of the aptly named Carl "Stubby" Mathias, who stood less than six feet tall, but weighed more than 200 pounds.

Nixon's single drove in Pete Runnels from second base. Runnels was in the game pinch-running for Wertz, which was like having a turtle pinch-run for a snail. The game winning hit was a grounder that hopped over the glove of Senators' second baseman Chuck Cottier.

"Every time I see Chuck, I remind him," said Nixon, who pinch-hit for Billy Harrell, who had pinch-hit for pitcher Ted Wills. "The thing about that inning was, sure, nobody expects to come back from seven runs down, but in those years, with the kind of explosive teams we had, all kinds of things happened at Fenway Park."

Pagliaroni's grand slam was the key to everything, and only part of a Bobby Thomson weekend. In the second game of the doubleheader, Pagliaroni hit a game-ending homer in the last of the 13th to give the Sox a 6-5 victory. On the day before the doubleheader, he hit a pinch home run as rookie pitcher Galen Cisco earned his first big-league win.

The memory of that comeback never left Sisler.

"I felt so badly about what happened," he said, "that shortly after that, they were picking the All-Star team, and they had to pick at least one player from each team and they had asked Dick Donovan from ours, but he was hurt—so they asked me instead.

"Well, they were gonna have a game in Boston [there were two All-Star games in 1961] and I told them there was no way I would go back to Boston as an All-Star after what happened, that I wouldn't go until I deserved it."

Sisler never was an All-Star, and all because of the greatest comeback in Red Sox history.

The play by play of that fateful ninth inning:

Wertz grounded to second. Buddin singled to left. Harrell, pinch-hitting for Wills, struck out. Schilling singled to left, Buddin to third. Hardy singled to center, Buddin scored, Schilling to second. Geiger walked, bases loaded. Sisler relieved Mathias. Jensen walked, Schilling scored, bases loaded. Malzone walked, Hardy scored, bases loaded. Pagliaroni homered into the screen (12-12), Geiger, Jensen and Malzone scored. Wertz walked. Kutyna relieved Sisler. Buddin singled to center, Wertz to second. Runnels pinch-ran for Wertz. Nixon, pinch-hitting for Harrell, singled to right, Runnels scored. *Eight runs*.

# Interlude:
# From the Bleachers
# to the Press Box

THERE IS A THEORY, AMONG THOSE WHO STUDY SUCH THINGS, that all of the pet cats with double paws in North America have ancestors that came over on the Mayflower.

Chances are that geneticists could do the same sort of detective work to explain why being a Red Sox fan seems to be an inherited trait. There has never been any natural advantage to it, or at least there wasn't from 1919 to 2003, a span of years just one short of four score and seven.

When people find out that someone goes to baseball games for a living, the most common reaction is:

1) It's the greatest job in the world, and

2) They'd do it for nothing.

The first assumption is absolutely correct, and a look at the average baseball writer's pay stub would indicate that the second one isn't far off. Essentially, all baseball writers started as fans and at some point in time evolved from paying to get in to being paid to get in.

For me, the very first step happened on the night of August 28, 1959, when I was seven.

It had been a warm day and remained a warm night, and some

time after going to bed I woke up thirsty. The only place to get a drink was downstairs, in the kitchen, and as I walked through the living room my dad was still awake and had the Red Sox game on TV. Anxious to delay returning to bed, I asked him if I could watch the rest of the game with him.

"Sure," he replied. "It's the last inning and Dick Gernert's up for the Red Sox. He's either gonna strike out, or hit a home run. Either way, the game will be over."

Gernert hit the next pitch into the screen that used to loom over the left-field wall. The game was over, I was convinced my father knew everything about baseball, and I was hooked on the Red Sox.

Years later, in 1988, I met Dick Gernert. He was scouting for the Mets and I was in Plant City, Florida, covering a Red Sox spring training game with the Reds. Gernert was a large man for his time, a typical Boston player of the day, big, strong and slow, and 29 years after he hit the home run that made me into a baseball fan, he was still big and strong.

He was also reputed to be one of the nicest men in the game, so I wandered over and introduced myself, then told him the story about how he was responsible for my being where I was at that moment.

"Do you have any idea how old that makes me feel?" Gernert said before beginning a most pleasant discussion of that home run—it was against the Orioles, off of Billy Loes, in the bottom of the 10th, and was the last one of his Red Sox career—and other related topics.

As much as I wanted to see the Red Sox in person after watching Gernert beat the Orioles on TV, the 1959 season was almost over by then, school was starting in a week, and there was no chance to actually get into Fenway Park. In 1960, though, that changed.

Ted Williams' career was winding down in 1960, but he was still a tremendous hitter and was making his final season a memorable one. So we went in to see Williams—it was one of those "You can tell your kids you saw Ted Williams play" things—on July 22, 1960. My memory is not sharp enough that I remembered the specific date. What I do remember is that Williams stole second base in the game, and that made looking up the date really easy.

The steal came in the seventh inning of a 6-4 victory over the Indians in front of a crowd of 29,595. In the first inning, Williams came up with two out and nobody on and homered off of Mudcat Grant, so I can tell my kids I saw Ted Williams hit a home run the first time I ever saw him swing a bat.

That notion of a player being so good you'd take your children in to see him play, just so they could tell *their* children you had seen him play, stuck with me, and remains with me today. It is my definition of a Hall of Fame player, and very few players ever meet that standard. Now, I have a vote for the Hall of Fame, and if a player doesn't pass that test—the buy a ticket just to say you saw him play test—he does not get my vote.

Which is why I don't vote for many players for the Hall of Fame.

Williams was gone after the 1960 season, and with him went much of the reason for going to Red Sox games. The Sox had been a lousy team throughout the 1950s, but at least Williams provided a diversion. With him gone, there was little to recommend them as entertainment, at least not for the serious baseball fan.

One benefit of that was that it was easy to get tickets, and the tickets were cheap. I remember on August 10, 1965, my father came home from work and decided we'd go to a game, just like that. Actually, go to a game and a half, since the Sox were playing a twi-night doubleheader against the Orioles.

When we left the house, Baltimore had just come up to bat in the top of the fifth inning of the first game. When we got to Fenway, the fifth inning was still going on. The Red Sox had scored 12 runs in their half of the inning on the way to a 15-5 win.

Jim Lonborg pitched a complete game, and we bought box seats for three dollars each and sat six rows from the field. The Orioles won the second game, but it really didn't matter. It was major league baseball about 50 feet from your nose and even in 1965, three dollars was a bargain price.

One of the fringe benefits of covering baseball is getting to meet players you watched as a fan. Actually, sometimes it's a fringe bene-fit. Other times it is a major disappointment. Getting to meet Lonborg, one of the major architects of the Sox' Impossible Dream in 1967, was definitely a fringe benefit.

Lonborg is one of the most articulate, approachable, personable people ever to wear a Boston uniform. In a conversation with him once, I reminded him of that Orioles doubleheader game, and in another breath, wondered if he could shed some light on a question that no one had ever been able to answer.

In the 1960s, I remembered, the respective starting pitchers would warm up before the game right in front of the box seats. There was a rubber, and an auxiliary home plate, between the near end of the dugout and the screen behind the real home plate.

The question was, when did Red Sox starting pitchers stop warm-ing up in front of the box seats?

"That's an easy one," Lonborg replied. "I was the last pitcher to warm up there, before the seventh game of the World Series in 1967. They took it out the next year and we had to warm up in the bullpen after that. I remember that we had a mound there, but it was a real-ly low mound, probably so someone wouldn't trip over it going after a foul ball."

The Impossible Dream changed everything, and for the better. That fact that the 2005 Red Sox play before capacity crowds at every Fenway game, and can sell box seats for $85, all goes back to 1967. It is as tangible a boundary as the Cape Cod Canal.

Nearly 40 years after the Impossible Dream, and nearly 20 after I started going to games for a living, seeing someone from 1967 still excites me. I have a copy of that 1967 Red Sox media guide and over the years have had players sign their profiles in that guide, a little booklet about the size of a business envelope. It isn't the autographs that mean so much as it is the stories that go along with them.

Dan Osinski, for instance.

Osinski was middle reliever for the 1967 Sox and had a good year in a limited role. He went 3-1, but middle relief may not have been his most important contribution to achieving the Impossible Dream. Osinski was a very strong man, perhaps the strongest on the team. When any of his teammates got into slumps, be they with the bat or on the mound, they were free to go to Osinski for treatment, which consisted of having the needy teammate place his head in the crook of Osinski's powerful right arm. The pitcher would then squeeze his teammate's head until he couldn't take it any more. This, Osinski said, would result in having any thoughts that led to the slump being forced out of the player's mind.

And all along fans thought that Lonborg and Yastrzemski were mainly responsible for making the Impossible Dream happen.

The Impossible Dream was fulfilled on October 1, 1967. In the afternoon, Rico Petrocelli caught Rich Rollins' pop-up to clinch at least a tie for first place. Years later, I asked Petrocelli what he did with the ball.

"I gave it to Lonborg," he said. "It was his game. He deserved it. But that could have been my vacation home in Florida. If only I knew."

Bill Landis was a southpaw relief pitcher in 1967 and like many players in those days, was in the Army Reserves. Landis was due to report for active duty during the summer, but was able to put it off, and put it off, and put it off as his team stayed in the pennant race. Finally, he could put if off no longer and had to report for duty starting October 1, the day of the 162nd game.

Landis was in fatigues in Louisiana when he found out his team had done the impossible.

As the years passed, Red Sox fans had to live mainly on Impossible Dream memories, but somehow the fortunes of the Boston franchise always seemed to be able to wind its tendrils around married, for instance, on October 11, 1975, the day of the Reds-Red Sox World Series.

At least the game didn't start until after the wed tion hall, however, was never quite full. There was a television downstairs and as the game went on, and the Sox kept building their lead, the crowd around the TV often outnumbered the crowd doing the chicken dance.

Our honeymoon ended on the night of October 21—late that night—and after a long drive my wife Debbie and I were tired and ready for bed. She turned in first. I had turned the TV on briefly and saw that Boston was behind, 6-3, in the eighth with Bernie Carbo up. I'd head for bed as soon as Carbo went out to end the inning, I said.

Another fringe benefit of writing about baseball, rather than merely watching it, is the chance to play a little of it once in a while. When Joe Morgan, then Butch Hobson, managed the Red Sox, it was OK for interested writers—on road trips, anyway—to come to the ballpark early and shag fly balls during early batting practice.

That was a time several hours before the game started in which players who had been hurt, or who were in a slump, or who had not been playing much, to get in some extra swings. There were usually five or six such players and if there were writers interested in standing around in the outfield to catch the occasional fly ball from Randy Kutcher, that was fine.

It was at one of these sessions that Gary Allenson, then Hobson's third base coach, told me that I was a pretty good fielder, but had the worst arm on a living human being he had ever seen. Allenson, who agreed with me that *It Happens Every Spring* is the best baseball movie ever made, was right.

In Baltimore's Camden Yards one day, infielder Jody Reed wandered over to a group of us and said he really enjoyed watching us

.g flies, purely for the entertainment value. "It looks like you're trying to catch watermelons dropped from the Goodyear Blimp," Reed added.

Shagging had some value beyond the pure joy of catching baseballs, though. It often opened up windows into the personalities of players who might be different in unguarded moments than they were when they knew someone was watching.

In 1990, Cleveland had yet to open either Jacobs Field or the Rock 'n' Roll Hall of Fame and there was not a lot to do downtown. Old Municipal Stadium was a popular shagging spot because it allowed for the killing of time, and it was always sort of a kick to catch fly balls in front of 72,000 empty seats. One hot day in the summer of 1990, I went over to shag and found the usual crew there—Kutcher, Mike Marshall, Luis Rivera, Kevin Romine—and for a change, Dwight Evans.

Evans was in center field chit-chatting when I trotted out to left. Third base coach Rac Slider was along the third base line hitting fungoes to anyone who was interested and not much happened until Marshall hit a fly ball to left that I caught.

Evans looked over and realized who was in left field and moved a bit in that direction. For the next 15 minutes, any time a ball was hit my way, Evans would sprint over from left-center like a Willie Mays impersonator and grab it before it got to me. Seeing this, Slider began hitting fungoes my way. Evans would race over and catch them, too.

Eventually, Evans got tired of showing me up and trotted off the field towards the Red Sox clubhouse. As Evans crossed the foul line, a disgusted Slider shook his head and spit on the ground. Evans finished the 1990 season with a .249 average and was not re-signed by the Sox. He claimed he had plenty of baseball left in him and went to Baltimore for one final, dreary season and probably wasn't there long enough for anyone to get a good read on the type of person behind the Hollywood smile.

The shagging ended in Seattle in 1993. The Mariners were still playing at the Kingdome then and shared the ugly, gray, concrete kettle with the NFL Seahawks. The football visitors locker room was kept open and that made it a perfect place to shower and change after a shagging session.

In the first week of July 1993 the Red Sox opened a West Coast trip in Seattle and I was joined at a shagging session by Sean Horgan of the *Hartford Courant*, the best athlete among all of the writers who covered Boston baseball. After early batting practice was done, we headed for the football locker room to get ready to go to work, something we had done for several years.

The locker room looked a bit different than we had remembered, but the showers and changing room were still there, so we undressed and walked over to the showers. But before Horgan could turn the water on, we heard the sound of a door opening, followed quickly by the sound of voices—many voices.

I peeked around the corner and saw a tour group—a couple of dozen tourists, cameras hanging from their necks—and they were stopping in the spare locker room to have some sort of a box lunch. The only way we could get to our clothes, or even our towels, was to walk right through the middle of the iced teas and tuna sandwiches, and that did not seem to be a viable option. So, instead, we pressed ourselves against the far wall of the shower room, saying silent prayers that none of the tourists would be curious enough to explore beyond the wooden benches they sat on to have lunch.

None were, but it was a very long 20 minutes of wondering exactly what the police report would look like if anyone had happened upon us.

By 1993, I was 41 anyway and it was time to hang up the glove, and towel.

As the years have passed, and New England has unconditionally surrendered its consciousness to the Red Sox, more and more people cover the team on a regular basis. Because of that, the chances to get to know players, coaches and managers on a one-to-one basis are disappearing, and that's progress, or what passes for it.

There are still the occasional thrills—getting to talk to John Glenn when the Sox held a tribute for Williams after his death—and the game itself remains infinitely interesting and unpredictable. The front row of the press box is still the domain of the regular beat writers, and the ongoing verbal sparring and wisecracking make it a nightly version of Cooperstown Squares. That sort of thing never gets old.

Sometimes, though, I wonder what would have happened if Dick Gernert had struck out.

# SNAPSHOT

## The Impossible Month

Take the Red Sox 1967 season, distill it into three weeks of unrelenting success, and there you have Lu Clinton, 1962.

Until June 28, 1962, Clinton was an underachieving Red Sox outfielder known mostly for one strange play on August 9, 1960 in Cleveland, when a ball hit by Indians first baseman Vic Power bounced off of the right field fence, hit Clinton in the foot, and bounced back over the stands for a home run.

As of June 28, 1962, nothing had happened to overshadow that moment.

Clinton was the lousiest player on a lousy team. Through June 28 he was hitting exactly .100, having gone 6 for 60 with one home run and seven RBIs. On June 29, though, manager Mike Higgins put Clinton in the starting lineup for a game against the Kansas City Athletics at Fenway Park. Boston had a 2-1 lead when Clinton, batting seventh, came up in the sixth. He hit a grand slam to give the Sox a 6-1 lead, then belted a two-run homer in the eighth and made it 9-3.

That was only the beginning.

Clinton stayed in the lineup, playing right field, and batting mostly seventh. Over a 19-game stretch that began on June 28, he put together perhaps the hottest long-term batting streak the Red Sox had ever seen, or would ever see.

The highlights:

In a July 4 doubleheader at Fenway versus the Twins, Clinton went 7 for 8 with two doubles and two home runs. He missed hitting for the cycle by one hit, a triple, in both games. In the second game, his two-run homer in the second gave the Sox a 2-1 lead; he singled and scored in the fourth to make it 4-1; he had an RBI double in the fifth to make it 5-1; and he singled and scored in the seventh to make it 8-5. Clinton was 12 for 15 in a four-game series with Minnesota that concluded with that doubleheader.

On July 7 in Los Angeles against the Angels, Clinton's three-run homer in the fourth was the key hit in a 5-4 Boston victory.

On July 12, in the second game of a doubleheader at Kansas City, Clinton homered in the second to make it 1-0, homered in the fifth to make it 2-1 and hit a two-run double in the top of the 11th to give the Sox a 6-4 lead in a game they eventually won, 9-4.

The next night, Clinton hit for the cycle as Boston won, 11-10, in 15 innings. His single in the top of the 15th drove in what proved to be the winning run. He was 5 for 7 with a walk, four runs scored and four RBIs.

On July 20, his bases-loaded triple in the first inning was the key hit in Boston's 8-4 victory over the White Sox at Fenway Park.

And that was it, although it was more than enough.

Clinton went 0 for 4 the next night and was 5 for 36 over the next 10 games. He finished the season batting .294 with 18 homers and 75 RBIs. Clinton hit 22 homers in 1963, but batted just .232. He was traded to the Angels for Lee Thomas in 1964 and bounced around the American League for a couple more years.

He finished his career with the Yankees in 1967, just as the Red Sox were rewriting their franchise history. Clinton settled in Wichita, Kansas where he ran a heating oil business, and where he died young in 1997, just 60 years old.

Clinton's memorable streak lasted for 19 games, during which he went 38 for 76 (.500), scored 25 runs and drove in 29. Clinton had seven doubles, four triples and nine home runs. His slugging percentage was 1.053, his on-base average .537. During the peak of the streak, nine games starting on July 3, he was 24 for 41 (.585).

# A Touch of Morgan Magic
## The 1987 and 1988 Seasons

THE RED SOX HAD NEVER BEEN COMFORTABLE, IT SEEMED, AS defending American League champions. They had followed up the 1946 pennant by finishing 14 games out in 1947. They were 17 games out in 1968 and barely broke the .500 mark in 1976.

No wonder that it seemed as if 1987 was a doomed season from the start.

It was my first year covering the team and my first impression was—how did they ever win anything in 1986? Manager John McNamara was an unpleasant man, the Henry Aaron of bad moods, whose affection for someone was in direct proportion to whatever Mac thought that person could do for him. Roger Clemens, who pitched the Sox to the pennant in 1986, held out in spring training and his catcher, Rich Gedman, was a free agent frozen out by a group of owners who were later found guilty of collusion.

Unable to curb their appetite for spending, baseball's owners decided to simply not take part in the annual free-agent market during the winter of 1987-88. It wasn't a bad idea, except that it was against the terms of their basic agreement with the players, who took their case to arbitration and won. Gedman wound up with a lot of money in the end, but his career was never the same.

Both players, Clemens and Gedman, eventually came back, but the 1987 Red Sox who opened the season in Milwaukee did so with—of all people—Bob Stanley on the mound and a catching tandem of Marc Sullivan and Danny Sheaffer.

Any hope Boston had of returning to the World Series was over early. The Sox' starters to being the season were Stanley, Al Nipper and Jeff Sellers, with ace Bruce Hurst held out to pitch the home opener at Fenway. Boston lost all three games to the Brewers, then Hurst shut out Toronto on April 10 at home. After the game, McNamara was asked if he had any regrets about waiting so long to use Hurst and spat out "That's a poorly worded question" for an answer.

The Brewers went 12-0 to start the year; by April 30, Boston was 9 ½ games out of first place and going nowhere. Clemens came back after an abbreviated spring training and lost his first start, 11-1, then went on to win 20 games and his second straight Cy Young Award. Gedman returned on May 2 and was 0 for 17, then 1 for 31, to begin his season.

In a scheduling quirk, the Sox played the Mets in a charity exhibition game at Shea Stadium on May 7. It was an eerie return to the place where Boston had suffered such immense disappointment the previous October. As a whole, the Sox just went about the business of playing the game and getting back to Fenway as quickly as possible. Bill Buckner, still getting used to his role, however unfair, as the goat of the 1986 World Series, made his entrance onto the playing field by shouting at reporters, "I had Mookie [Wilson] hit me ground balls before the game."

It was sad, actually.

There was little of the 1986 Sox in the 1987 version. McNamara got a hall pass by virtue of winning the pennant the year before, but it was a difficult year for him. McNamara was enamored with veteran players like Buckner and Don Baylor, but the 1987 team was one in transition and the Boston farm system sent a bountiful harvest of potentially good young players to Fenway.

Baylor, Buckner and Dave Henderson—the hero of the 1986 play-offs—were all gone before the end of the season. Age caught up with Baylor and Buckner. Henderson was hobbled by injuries and seemed disinterested when he did play. He was traded to the Giants for Randy Kutcher and then the Giants got rid of him. It wasn't until he arrived in Oakland that Henderson finally blossomed as an every-day player.

As the season went on, six newcomers arrived from Triple A in center fielder Ellis Burks, pitcher Tom Bolton, catcher John Marzano, DH Sam Horn, utility player Todd Benzinger and shortstop Jody Reed. The young players—especially Burks, who was the best all-around athlete to wear a Boston uniform since Jackie Jensen—made the season interesting, at least for fans. But not for McNamara.

His attitude towards rookies was vividly demonstrated in the person of first baseman Pat Dodson, a powerful left-handed batter who had shown some promise in a brief big-league stint in 1986. The rap on Dodson was that he had a slow bat—could not catch up with a good fastball—and that probably was true. But he was the best defensive first baseman the Boston organization had produced since George Scott in the 1960s.

But McNamara did not see it that way. One day in Cleveland, after a discussion involving Dodson's playing time, McNamara gave the standard answers, then pulled aside a couple of reporters and told them about the slow bat theory. Beyond that, McNamara added, "The man is not that good defensively. He's one of those guys who likes making routine plays look hard."

The season ended on October 4 with Clemens throwing a 4-0 shutout at the Brewers, giving him 20 wins and back to back shutouts. He was the Cy Young winner and Wade Boggs won the batting title, but the season was bitterly disappointing beyond that. In the off-season, Gorman made a fabulous trade, sending Nipper and Calvin Schiraldi to the Cubs in exchange for reliever Lee Smith. With that one move, the Red Sox became contenders again.

The expectations for 1988 were substantial and there were higher expectations as spring training opened, something McNamara found disturbing. At one point, in talking about his team's prospects for 1988, he turned a pleasant enough discussion into another miserable chat by glaring at *Boston Globe* reporter Dan Shaughnessy—who had written that Boston would win the AL East title—and saying that things were going well enough except "When somebody picks you to finish first to get you [expletive] fired."

Even the Red Sox public relations department was not immune to the atmosphere of paranoia engendered by McNamara. Late in spring training, a visiting reporter grabbed lunch in the tiny press dining room and walked out the door with a half-eaten hamburger in his hand.

PR assistant Josh Spofford tore out the door after the poor man, grabbed the burger from his hand and screamed at him that no one was allowed to take food from the dining room. The reporter stuttered that he didn't know and was sorry, but Spofford continued the tirade as if the unfortunate guy was trying to swipe a Gutenberg Bible. The odd thing was that almost nobody who watched the scene was surprised—that was just the way the Red Sox treated people in those days.

The season opened at Fenway Park with Smith serving up a 10th-inning home run to Detroit's Alan Trammell in a 5-3 loss. The headline in the *Boston Herald* on the day after read "Wait 'Till Next Year."

Smith, and the Sox, survived the opening-day defeat and Boston played fairly well in April but began to sag as the weather warmed up. Dwight Evans had become the regular first baseman with Benzinger working in occasionally. The rookie was hurt a lot, though, and McNamara had little use for him. The situation boiled over in Anaheim in late May when the manager was doing a pre-game interview in the dugout, with Evans sitting a few feet away listening in.

When it was suggested that Evans go back to right field and Benzinger be installed at first, Evans walked over to the group and said, "So you want to move me? Who's going to play first? The man [Benzinger] is always hurt. How is he going to play first base if he's always hurt? How can you put him in the lineup? What are you going to do—move everybody around to cater to him?"

As Evans left, McNamara just smiled and said, "I didn't say that."

The Red Sox slipped below .500 in mid-June and the public demand to fire McNamara had become so loud it was threatening to drown out the season. In Baltimore, with his team 8 ½ games out of first, McNamara summoned reporters to his office for an unexpected pre-game announcement. The manager despised the media, so it had to be something major, perhaps his resignation. Instead, McNamara read a convoluted prepared statement saying that he would no longer answers questions about his job situation.

The session began with an unforgettable piece of rhetoric, McNamara saying, "There have been no ultimations."

Within days, a story broke about Boggs' affair with a West Coast woman named Margo Adams. On a plane trip to Cleveland, somebody—it was never proven to be catcher Rick Cerone—let off a stink bomb. When the Sox finally arrived at the ancient Hollenden House, their hotel, there was something resembling a fight. It was the Fall of Rome minus Hannibal and the elephants and the bewildered, besieged McNamara was powerless to do anything about it.

On July 10, Boston played its final game before the All-Star break, rookie Steve Curry losing to the White Sox at Comiskey Park. Curry had been a great Triple A pitcher, but that never translated at the big-league level. His major Red Sox legacy was in his recuperation from subsequent arm surgery. Curry's doctor told him that while he could not do very much with his right arm in the first couple of weeks after the operation, he at least could sit in front of the TV and flex his arm while holding a can of Campbell's Soup.

On a follow up visit, Curry was asked if he had been able to work his arm using the soup-can technique. Oh yes, Curry replied, but I had to stop after a few days.

Alarmed, the surgeon asked why.

"My wife cooked the soup," Curry answered.

The end came for McNamara on Bastille Day—July 14, 1988. His firing was handled so poorly that it was almost possible to feel sympathetic towards the old grouch—almost, but not quite.

Ownership had let McNamara stew about his future through the All-Star break, and had gone so far as to actually let him drive into Fenway Park from his home in South Natick, then fill out a lineup card for that night's scheduled game with the Royals. There are two doors to the manager's office at Fenway Park—one that leads into the clubhouse, and a side door that opens onto the corridor that leads to the players' parking lot. About three hours before game time, the door to the clubhouse closed and the side door opened for Gorman and minority owner Haywood Sullivan, McNamara's friend.

And with that, Mac was gone.

The press conference and formal announcement came a bit later. The way that many found out about it was by simply looking at the door that opened into the clubhouse. The name on it "McNamara" had been clumsily covered over by black electrical tape, like a sheet drawn over a body, with the outline of the name underneath still quite obvious. Below it, in equally clumsy fashion, a few magnetic letters had been stuck to the door in the form of "Morgan."

The Sox hired third base coach Joe Morgan as interim manager, the idea being that he would do until a bigger, more experienced name could be found. The one that came up most often was Joe Torre, who had last managed in the majors in 1984. Until then, Morgan would be a good transitional guy. After all, Boston was tied for fourth in the AL East, nine games behind first-place Detroit. The rest of the 1988 season was going to be spring training for 1989.

But it was an eerily confident Morgan who took over on July 14. At the age of 57, he had given up hope of ever managing in the majors. Morgan had spent years in the minor leagues, most of them at Triple A, and had never made more than $23,000 a year down there. Until being rewarded with post-season bonus money from Boston's 1986 season, Morgan had worked winter jobs, the most recent being on the road crew for the Massachusetts Turnpike, where he had helped the Commonwealth dig out from the Blizzard of 1978.

When team president John Harrington approached Morgan about taking over for McNamara, part of the new manager's reply was, "Mr. Harrington, the word 'interim' is not in my vocabulary."

Right after being hired, if only for a while, Morgan headed out the door of his new office to make sure everyone knew what had happened. On the field, bullpen coach Rac Slider was hitting ground balls to Boggs; McNamara's treatment of Slider was an example of how McNamara had operated.

The bullpen coach had spent decades as a minor league manager for Boston, most of that time in the blazing hellholes of the low minors. Finally, in 1987, Slider was promoted to the big leagues in the form of bullpen coach. McNamara essentially ignored Slider for a year and a half until, finally, he could sense his bullpen coach's simmering resentment. So, on the afternoon of July 14, just back from the All-Star break, McNamara invited Slider into his office for a perfunctory talk.

As Slider walked out one door, management walked in the other. While the managerial change was taking place, Slider was out on the field, oblivious to the shaking of the ground in the clubhouse. When Morgan sauntered out onto the field to tell Slider he was the new manager, Slider at first thought it was a joke. He couldn't believe that the first time McNamara talked with him turned out to be his last act as manager.

Morgan wound up having to wait a day to make his debut behind a major-league bench. The game that night was rained out and rescheduled as part of a doubleheader the next day, with Clemens pitching Game One.

Clemens was overpowering in a performance that ranked with the best games he ever pitched in a Red Sox uniform. Clemens beat Bret Saberhagen and the Royals, 3-1, striking out 16. The Sox won the second game, 7-4, and Part Two of the 1988 season had begun very well.

What came to be known as Morgan's Magic started the next afternoon, a warm Saturday at Fenway Park.

Boston played Kansas City in the third game of their four-game series. The Royals hammered Sox starter Oil Can Boyd and had a 6-0 lead after five innings. But the Red Sox got four runs in the last of the sixth and Evans tied it with a two-run homer in the bottom of the eighth. In the last of the ninth, Kevin Romine was due to lead off for Boston. Morgan had slugger Larry Parrish on the bench as a possible pinch-hitter, but sent Romine out to bat anyway. Romine was, at the time, hitting .154 and had never, ever hit a home run in 127 major-league at bats.

This time, he took Strike One from Royals reliever Steve Farr, then hit the next pitch on a sharp line into the screen above the Green Monster. Boston 7, Kansas City 6, and something seemed to be happening with the rejuvenated Red Sox.

They made it a sweep of the Royals the next day, then greeted the Twins at Fenway for more of the supernatural. On July 19, Mike Smithson took a no-hitter into the seventh and Boston won, 5-0. That made it six in a row, enough for management to remove the "interim" from Morgan's title. It was now not in anybody's vocabulary. Signed for at least the duration of the 1988 season, Morgan took over as permanent manager on July 20. His team celebrated by playing one of the most illogically dramatic, emotional games in franchise history.

Clemens started and had a 5-0 lead through five innings. Minnesota came back and made it 5-4 in the top of the eighth. In the bottom of the eighth, Boston had Ellis Burks on first base with one out and Jim Rice due up. Morgan called Rice back from the on-deck circle and sent up backup shortstop Spike Owen to pinch-hit. Or at least, to pinch-bunt, which is what Owen did successfully. When Rice returned to the dugout he yelled at the new manager and shoved him, to which Morgan responded, "I'm the skipper of this nine."

Fans around the dugout could hear the commotion and craned their necks to see what was going on, but the altercation was in the runway leading to the clubhouse. Other Sox players broke it up and the game went on, although Rice was later suspended by the team for three games.

While Owen got the bunt down successfully, Burks never scored and the Twins eventually came back to tie it at 5-5 in the ninth. Minnesota then scored twice in the top of the 10th and it was 7-5 and once again, Morgan's Magic seemed to have reached its end.

While the Twins were rallying, circumstances were evolving that would bring Boston an improbable victory. Over in the third-base grandstand a fan had climbed up one of the support poles for Fenway's ancient roof. He then clambered out onto the guide wire that extended all the way down to the screen behind home plate and supported the screen from the third-base side. Then slowly, deliberately, the fan began to shinny down the wire towards the screen, hand over hand, his feet wrapped around the wire, his body hanging over the box seats below.

On the mound was Minnesota reliever Juan Berenguer. Berenguer, a right-hander, had to look directly at the descending fan every time he stopped to set in his motion. By now, Fenway Park was buzzing as some 33,000 or so people watched the trapeze show going on over the visitors dugout. No one in the ballpark tried to stop the acrobat. The umpires did not stop the game. For his part, Berenguer could not keep his eyes off of the sideshow. He would look at the man on the wire, look at home plate, and throw a pitch. A pitch that was almost always a ball.

Berenguer walked Mike Greenwell, got an out, then walked Owen. Shaken, Berenguer finally walked off the mound and was replaced by Keith Atherton. Jody Reed greeted Atherton with a double off the wall to make it 7-6. Todd Benzinger followed Reed to the plate, worked the count to 2 and 2, and then hooked a majestic fly ball around Pesky's Pole in right for a game-winning home run.

Boston 9, Minnesota 7.

The White Sox came to Fenway for four games and they were

swept, too. On July 21, Boyd took a perfect game into the seventh and Boston won, 6-1. On July 24, a Sunday afternoon, Smith came on in the eighth with a one-run lead and struck out four of the five Chicago batters he faced to save a 3-2 victory that concluded an 11-0 homestand.

As the streak continued, Morgan went from having the best start to a Red Sox' managerial career to the best start of any managerial career in baseball history, and the entire nation began to take notice. In a sport where ego and pay stubs had begun to define its most visible figures, Morgan was just the opposite. He would autograph baseballs with the names of dead presidents, toss them into the stands and watch the reaction as some fan read "Chester A. Arthur" on his official American League ball. One time, Morgan did that and a little girl, about 10 or so, got a "Grover Cleveland" ball. She began to cry and Morgan felt so bad that he had her come into the dugout, gave her a ball, and instructed all of the Red Sox players sitting there to sign it.

In Baltimore one time, Morgan discovered that he and Shaughnessy both had gift certificates from the same clothing store for doing local radio appearances. Shaughnessy was headed downtown to cash his in and Morgan figured he could have the writer take his, too, and redeem it, so Shaughnessy soon found himself bringing $75 worth of boxer shorts back to Morgan's room at the Cross Keys Inn.

The door to Morgan's office was always open and you never knew who would be in there. At Fenway, his post-game press meetings would often end with him saying, "OK, Anthony, you can come out now" and his grandson would pop out from under the desk where he had been hiding all along. One night Reggie Jackson would be in Morgan's office talking about who baseball's best clutch hitters were, and the next night Morgan would have a couple of farmers from Mansfield in there, men who provided him with manure for his backyard garden, and they would be discussing just how much rain tomato plants needed.

One afternoon in 1991, with Fenway Park playing host to an old-timers get together, *Hartford Courant* reporter Sean Horgan remembered that he had told Morgan to get him a baseball so he could scrounge some autographs. Horgan hurried into the manager's office and there, sitting at an angle to each other with Morgan's desk in the middle, were the manager, Ted Williams, and Carl Yastrzemski. Williams and Yastrzemski were debating the science of hitting. Or, more accurately, Williams was bellowing—this was not because he was angry, since Williams would bellow out the Lord's Prayer—and Yastrzemski was listening. Horgan could hear one phrase being repeated with each point Williams made to Yaz—"You dumb Polack." Realizing that this was a once-in-a-lifetime confluence of baseball planets, Horgan flipped the ball to Williams and he signed it without halting his relentless assault on Yastrzemski's hearing.

Visitors to the office, especially from July on, would be asked to look into one of the drawers in the manager's desk and pick out some Walpole-grown vegetables to take home with them, a souvenir of their trip to Fenway Park.

Williams had become a Morgan fan and was always welcome in the manager's office, but so was someone like Jack Ratcliffe, who played for Whitinsville against Morgan's Hopedale team in the old Blackstone Valley League in the early 1950s. Ratcliffe kept a stack of scrapbooks from the BVL days and Morgan would invite him in and talk about Alex Nahigian and Chewy Lucier and Hop Riopel until it was almost game time.

Morgan loved baseball history, and loved talking to players from the past, and knew that I did, too. One afternoon in Seattle's old Kingdome, he hollered to me to come in as I was walking past his office on the way out of the clubhouse. He was talking to a couple of older men, then turned and asked me, "What can you tell me about a pitcher named Jack Wilson?"

I replied, "Jack Wilson is considered to be one of the worst pitchers in Red Sox history." And Morgan responded, "Well, say hi to him because he's sitting right there in that chair."

Wilson, whom I had confused with Jack Russell, was actually not all that bad for the Sox teams of the Jimmie Foxx era, and took my ill-advised remark with good humor, saying, "You must have seen me pitch."

The Red Sox are always a national story, and Morgan became a headliner as his record-breaking run as new manager continued. Near the end of that first Fenway homestand, he begun to tell reporters about an upcoming interview he had with a TV newsman, Dana Kiecker. We all knew that Dana Kiecker was a pitcher for the Pawtucket Red Sox; when Boston got to Texas for its first road trip under Morgan, he did an interview in the lobby of the Sheraton hotel in Arlington with NBC reporter Douglas Kiker.

The streak continued in Texas on July 25 when Clemens beat the Rangers, 2-0. The game, a night game, was played in 100-degree heat and Clemens threw an unimaginable 161 pitches. It was 96 when the game began, then climbed to 100 after sundown, which made no sense. Except to Slider, who had taken over as third base coach when McNamara was fired. Slider owned a ranch in northeast Texas, in DeKalb, where singer Rick Nelson had died in a plane crash a few years earlier. Slider explained that on the barren Texas plains, the ground absorbs the heat during the day, then radiates it back up after sundown. Thus, the decidedly un-New England phenomenon.

Boston's 12-game winning streak, its best since 1948, ended on July 26 in a 9-8 loss that left the Sox 2 ½ games out of first place. A venerable sports adage is that streaks follow streaks, so it seemed reasonable to expect Boston to come back to earth, Morgan's Magic or not.

That was hardly the case.

The Sox started a new winning streak the next night with Gardner getting the start on another brutally hot evening. Boston won, 10-7, though Gardner finally wilted in the seventh. He lived in Benton, Arkansas, and Texas was as close as he got to home during the season. The Red Sox were off the next day, so Gardner got permission to head home to visit his family. The pitcher got a little rest, then drove through the night and finally got to his parents' house early in the morning.

He parked the car and got out and was greeted by his father, who said nice to see you, son, the garden needs to be weeded and here's a hoe. Which is what Gardner did on his day off.

While Gardner was gardening, Gorman was lining up a major trade. With the Sox having unexpectedly jumped back into contention, Boston had become a trade market buyer, not seller. The Sox needed more starting pitching, as they always did; the Orioles had veteran Mike Boddicker to shop with and were looking for prospects to rebuild with.

Boston was back home on July 29 and had a doubleheader scheduled with the Brewers. It was a Friday, and the menu in the press dining room, where Red Sox executives also ate, included make-your-own sundaes. Gorman, however, was nowhere to be found at lunch time, and he especially loved dessert. There could be only one reason—a trade—and sure enough, the announcement was made later that afternoon. The Sox had acquired Boddicker for Brady Anderson, who had opened the 1988 season in center field, and minor league pitcher Curt Schilling.

All the while, Morgan's Magic continued. The 12-game streak was followed by a seven-game streak, making it 19 wins in 20 games. When Morgan took over, the Red Sox were nine games out of first place. On August 3, the Red Sox extended Morgan's contract through the end of the 1989 season, then they beat the Rangers at Fenway, 5-4, to move into a tie for the lead with Detroit. It had been a dizzying, unprecedented, exhausting, climb and of all things, the Tigers were next on the schedule.

Boston began a five-game series in Detroit on August 4. It proved to be the end of Morgan's Magic. After that, the season turned into a mere pennant race with all of the standard drama and pathos. The Red Sox eventually won it, but those days in Detroit made it painfully obvious that emotion and miracles both had shelf lives.

The Tigers won each of the first four games at Tiger Stadium. Boston was back where it had been just eight games into Morgan's Magic and the season was in danger of reverting to form. The Sox lost on Saturday, August 6 by 4-2. After the game, reporters filed into a silent Boston clubhouse and entered the manager's office, the smallest one in baseball, a tiny cubicle no bigger than the bathroom in a standard Hampton Inn.

As Morgan began to answer questions, the phone on his little desk rang. No one had ever heard the phone ring before—not Morgan, not even any of the reporters who had covered the team for a long time—and everyone assumed it was a wrong number. It kept ringing, so Morgan eventually picked it up. What ensued was a conversation straight from Bob Newhart.

"Hello.

"Yes, this is he. To whom might I be speaking?

"Dick Duncan, eh. Dick, how are you? What can I do for you?

"I understand, yes....you might be right...that's not a bad idea.

"Dick, you're calling at a bit of an inopportune time. I'm a little busy, but it was nice to hear from you.

"Thanks. You, too. Good-bye."

When he hung up, Morgan was asked who Dick Duncan was.

"Never heard of him before in my life," was the reply. What happened, it turned out, was that a Red Sox fan back home had called the Tiger Stadium switchboard and asked to speak to the manager— and was put through, no questions asked. Morgan handled the call and the ensuing advice with grace despite the fact that his team's season was on the verge of unraveling, then went on to take more questions.

The final question had to do with Sunday's game, and Boston's chances at avoiding a sweep with Bruce Hurst on the mound.

"Hurst'll spin a beauty," Morgan said. "We'll win tomorrow and leave here three games out."

The Tigers were horrified by what they perceived as Morgan's arrogance in predicting a victory. But he had managed Hurst in the minors, then joined him in the majors when he was promoted to a coaching position. Morgan thought that Hurst was one of the best big-game pitchers he had ever seen, and the lefty's performance in the 1986 post-season bore him out. So, on August 7, 1988, with the Sox in danger of falling five games out of first place, Hurst pitched a sensational 10-inning shutout and Boston won, 3-0.

Hurst and Jeff Robinson dueled through nine scoreless innings before the Sox rallied in the 10th. The key hit was an RBI single by Benzinger, deadly in the clutch again, and the game ended with Benzinger making a diving play at first base on a grounder, then feeding the ball to Hurst, who pumped his fist as he crossed the bag.

The rest of the stretch drive was, essentially, the standard pennant race war of attrition. Boston finally made up the ground lost in Detroit in early September and by the 14th had built a 4 ½ game lead. That was just in time for a four-game series with the Yankees, who arrived at Fenway Park on September 15 with the memories of 1978's Boston Massacre still very fresh.

They got fresher when New York won the first game of the series, but the Red Sox took the next three. First place was now theirs to lose, which they had done before, but this was a different team. They went into Yankee Stadium on September 23 with New York four games out. The Yankees had a 9-5 lead in the sixth when Boston staged a most memorable comeback. The Sox cut the lead to 9-7 heading into the ninth, then made it 9-8 and had the bases loaded with one out for Owen, who came up to pinch-hit for Edgardo Romero.

Owen chopped a grounder over the mound. It should have been a double play ball, but Yankees shortstop Wayne Tolleson and second baseman Willie Randolph could not decide who should make the play. Neither did, two runs scored, and Boston wound up with a 10-9 victory.

On the way up the ramp from the Sox dugout and into the clubhouse, the voice of veteran pitcher Bob Stanley, who had suffered through more defeats like that than victories, could be heard bellowing, "That game was a ripper. It ripped the hearts right out of them."

Boston took two out of three from the Yankees and the pennant race was over. So was the season, for that matter. The Red Sox lost six of their last seven games in the regular season, then were swept in four by the Athletics in the ALCS. It some sense, the post-season almost did not matter, much like in 1967. Morgan's arrival in mid-July had provided fans with a longer, far more entertaining summer than any of them had expected.

# SNAPSHOT

## The Funniest Man in Baseball

When Lou Gorman traded Spike Owen to the Expos in December of 1988, he got a starting pitcher, John Dopson, and a utility infielder in return. Gorman figured on that infielder, Luis Rivera, as good insurance. He didn't realize he had traded for the funniest man anyone around the Red Sox had ever known.

While Pedro Martinez was a clown, a slapstick character, Rivera was surgical with his humor. A native of Puerto Rico, given a different set of circumstances, Rivera could have been the Carson of the Caribbean. Instead, he was content to merely liven up the Boston clubhouse from the summer of 1989 through the end of the 1993 season.

Rivera did not grow up rich, but neither was he hungry as a kid back home. That's because his dad owned a grocery store. Mr. Rivera did a good business, but was not a good businessman. Customers would come in for groceries and if they didn't happen to have enough money to pay for them, Mr. Rivera simply let them take the food home and said "Pay me when you can."

Which usually was never.

Luis Rivera was signed as a 17-year-old by the Expos in 1981 and started playing in 1982 and once told a story about having to send most of his meager minor-league paychecks home.

"I was playing in Class A," Rivera remembered, "and I didn't want to spend any money, so I lived with some teammates, but didn't have a room of my own. I didn't want to spend money on a bed, so I'd roll up my clothes and sleep on them, on the floor."

I asked how long this went on, and Rivera said it went on for all the years he was making Class A money.

"How long were you in Class A?" I asked, and he said it was three years.

"A good prospect like you, in the major leagues at 22, and you spent three years playing Class A ball?"

"Of course," Rivera replied. "For those three years I never got any sleep."

Joe Morgan loved how Rivera played the game, and how he played hurt without complaining, but Butch Hobson was not of the same mind. During the two years Hobson managed Rivera, the shortstop was a part-timer. One day, after a benching that had lasted especially long, reporters headed over to Rivera's locker—it had become a mandatory stop each day—and saw a huge sign pasted over it.

"Will play for food."

When Rivera wasn't playing, he'd take a broom and trash bucket into the Red Sox dugout and sweep up. His locker, over in a corner created by the angle with the manager's office, was next to Roger Clemens and Jeff Russell. On the carpet of the clubhouse, Rivera taped a boundary line that he said could not be crossed. He taped down two arrows going in opposite directions, and some words. One arrow pointed in the direction of Russell and Clemens and read, "Texas—Rednecks." The other said "Mexico—Tacos."

When Scott Fletcher was with the Sox, he and Rivera got into a conversation about swimming, with Rivera revealing he could not swim. "How can you live on an island and not know how to swim?" asked Fletcher in disbelief. To which Rivera replied, "Easy. Get a boat."

Another time, team doctor Arthur Pappas made his daily stroll down the middle of the clubhouse. Pappas was a friendly man, but had eyebrows straight from the rain forest, and did not have the look of someone you'd want to tease.

Rivera did, anyway.

"Hey doc, you're looking good today. What did you do all day?" Rivera yelled over as Pappas headed towards the trainer's room.

"I operated on two people," the doctor responded.

"Oh, good," said Rivera. "Are they still alive?"

After Rivera's playing career ended, he stayed in the game as a manager in the Indians farm system. The paychecks weren't great, but at least he didn't have to sleep on the floor. And, in a pinch, there was always the possibility of a late-night TV gig.

# The Magic Ends

THE MALAISE THAT HAD BEGUN IN THE FINAL WEEK OF THE 1988 season lingered through the winter. The Red Sox arrived in Winter Haven for spring training, 1989, lacking focus and energy. The emotion that had carried them to an unlikely AL East title had long since evaporated.

On March 16, in an exhibition game against the Rangers at Port Charlotte, Boston lost, 10-4, and saw its Grapefruit League record fall to 3-9. As Morgan dressed near the end of the game, he blasted his players, saying, "I wish we were home right now so I could wake this dead-ass team up . . . Maybe this was a great game for us to see. Maybe this is just the game we need to wake our [foolish] dead asses up."

Except that waking up the Sox would have to wait for a day or two. Morgan had a plane to catch. He had agreed to fly home to Walpole to be grand marshal of the annual St. Patrick's Day parade. That's why he was leaving early.

The season was no better than spring training.

Boston opened in Baltimore, with President George H.W. Bush, the old Yale first baseman, throwing out the first ball. The Sox lost in 11 innings, 5-4, to the rejuvenated Orioles who had men at first and third and one out when Morgan decided to go with a five-man infield. Craig Worthington hit a fly ball to left-center that fell for a single in the semi-deserted outfield; it would have been a sacrifice fly anyway.

The Red Sox lost their first two games in Baltimore, then went to Kansas City. The tawdry hysteria surrounding Wade Boggs and his spurned, litigious, ex-lover Margo Adams was at its peak as the season opened. In Baltimore, fans paraded around the concourse holding signs that said "Hey Wade—we're not wearing any underwear" and at the gates to Royals Stadium in Kansas City, fans passed out pictures of Ms. Adams attached to sticks and called them Margo Masks. Reliever Mike Smithson, who on a daily basis commandeered the clubhouse TV for an hour of watching the Three Stooges, grabbed one and said he'd wear it in the bullpen.

During the previous winter, Gorman traded with the Reds and the Expos. He got first baseman Nick Esasky and reliever Rob Murphy from Cincinnati; pitcher John Dopson and shortstop Luis Rivera from Montreal. Esasky was one of the few bright spots in a dismal season. He had a career year before departing for his hometown of Atlanta. Murphy performed well, too, and was an island of articulate sanity and humor in a stormy season.

The last time Boston was in first place in 1989 was on May 12, when it had a 17-15 record. All anyone needed to know about 1989 happened on June 4, when the Sox played one of the most traumatic games in franchise history. They led Toronto, 10-0, after six innings and lost, 13-11, in 12 innings. The killer blow was Ernie Whitt's grand slam off of Lee Smith in the top of the ninth. To add injury to the ultimate insult, second baseman Marty Barrett tripped while running out a ground ball in the ninth, injuring his knee. Barrett's career essentially ended that day. He later sued the Sox, and team owner-doctor Arthur Pappas, claiming that Pappas misdiagnosed the extent of the knee injury, and won a judgment.

The season was the last one for veterans Jim Rice and Bob Stanley, and it got ugly at times, especially with Rice. His skills had clearly disappeared and his body was betraying him, too, at 36. By the end of the season Rice had been reduced to a bench player, and wound up making a graceless exit as had Barrett, who one day in Detroit railed against announcer Sean McDonough about something his father, *Globe* columnist Will McDonough, had written.

As the 1989 season wound down, Rice had an outburst in the clubhouse, complaining about how poorly the Sox, who had paid him $9,413,095 since 1985, treated their players. At the end, Rice shouted over towards Boggs, "Isn't that right, Boggsie?"

To which Boggs very calmly replied, "Actually, no. This organization has always treated me very well."

In early May, Boston signed free-agent pitcher Joe Price, a quiet left-hander who had had some good years in the National League, but was just about pitched out. Price, though, had an excellent perspective on things since he was new to the Red Sox. In talking about arriving in town, new and knowing hardly anyone on the team, Price stood at his locker and said, "I looked for leadership over there," nodding in the direction of where Rice dressed, "and then I looked for leadership over there," nodding towards Evans' locker, "and I found nothing."

Later in the season, on September 9, Price was involved in an incident that was symptomatic of how the team had drifted through the year. He was pitching in Anaheim against the Angels and walked the speedy Devon White in the sixth inning. White proceeded to steal his way around—second base, third base, then home—and after Price was lifted and began making his way up the tunnel to the Red Sox clubhouse, Morgan hollered after him, "Joe—why didn't you use your slide step?" Price's reply was unprintably rude and the Sox eventually suspended him for four days.

What else happened in 1989?

Boston released utility infielder Edgardo Romero on August 5. In making separate announcements, Gorman called him "Edgar," and Morgan called him "Eduardo." Neither knew Romero's real first name. In the clubhouse, as he cleaned out his locker, Romero asked reporters if they wanted any of his excess equipment. No one did, save for Jeff Horrigan of the *Manchester Union-Leader*. Horrigan had a headache and wanted Romero's little bottle of Advil, but only on one condition, that Romero autograph it. And he did.

On September 20 in Toronto's SkyDome, Mike Greenwell missed a game because he was run over by a utility tractor while playing catch before the game.

And on May 3 at Chicago's old Comiskey Park, Morgan broke with his scheme of platooning catchers Rich Gedman and Rick Cerone by starting Cerone, a right-handed hitter, against right-hander Shawn Hillegas. Cerone won the game with a two-run homer in the sixth.

Afterwards, in the manager's office, somebody asked Morgan about the pitching of Boddicker and Morgan replied, "That's not the story of this game. When I made out the lineup card, I was sure that Hillegas was a left-hander, so I put Cerone in there. When I found out he wasn't, I figured, "What the Hell. Leave him in there."

It turned out that Morgan had confused Hillegas with Chicago lefty Paul Kilgus. Beyond that, Cerone, thinking he would be getting a night off, didn't get back to his room until about 4 A.M. on the morning of the game.

Everybody was stunned that, not only would Morgan admit to such a mistake, but he would do it without being asked. When White Sox manager Jeff Torborg was told what had happened, and asked if he would do the same, Torborg replied, "I wouldn't have even told my wife."

That Morgan would own up to such a mistake was not out of character. After all, this was a manager who had been given his own TV show for the 1989 season and once asked a visitor if he had seen the show yet.

When the answer was yes, Morgan added, "Isn't it awful?"

The Sox put on a little run in September to at least finish above .500, but they had not fooled anyone. In the off-season, Gorman signed reliever Jeff Reardon and catcher Tony Pena as free agents, but that meant that Boston headed into 1990 with two closers. Eventually, one would have to go, and it was obviously going to be Smith.

Smith had been effective in his two seasons with the Sox, but for him, baseball was a one-way street. It was his way, or the highway. In spring training in 1989, the Sox had scheduled their pitching so that in one game at Winter Haven, Smith would work both the eighth and ninth innings. He came in for the eighth, then walked off of the mound and headed for the clubhouse without saying a word to anyone. Pitching coach Bill Fischer raced after him, flabbergasted, and hollered out, "Lee…Lee…what the [deuce]. You're supposed to pitch two."

Smith kept walking, shook his head, put up the index finger on his right hand and said, simply, "One, man." The Sox had to send down to the nearby minor-league complex and get a kid from there warmed up to finish the game.

Smith did not like being put into games where he could not get a save, and when he was, often showed his displeasure by throwing batting practice fastballs to opposition hitters. That was what happened in the awful 13-11 loss to Toronto where the Jays came back from 10 runs down. Smith was a no-show for Boston's Hall of Fame exhibition game in 1989, never bothering to tell anyone that he had no intention of making it to Cooperstown.

He was finally traded to St. Louis on May 4, 1990 in exchange for outfielder Tom Brunansky. In all, it was a very good deal for the Sox and part of a season that, in general, started very well.

Pena brought a lot of positive energy to clubhouse. He started the season hitting over .300 and was excellent defensively. He was in the middle of an incident in early June that seemed to serve as a catalyst for Boston's surge into first place.

On June 1 in Cleveland, the Red Sox trailed the Indians—managed by John McNamara—by a 3-2 score with two out and nobody on base in the top of the ninth and Tribe stopper Doug Jones on the mound. Boston took the lead in a span of three pitches—Dwight Evans singled, Pena tripled him home, then Mike Greenwell singled. The Sox hung on to win, 4-3, and after the game, the Indians hosted an evangelical session for youngsters out in the bleachers, with Jones as the main speaker, telling the kids about the virtues of loving thy neighbor, etc.

So, on Saturday, June 2 with the Indians on their way to a 7-5 victory, Pena came up to hit in the top of the ninth and Jones showed his love by throwing a fastball at the Boston catcher's left ear. Pena hit the dirt and got out of the way, but after the game told reporters, "Somebody's going down tomorrow."

That somebody was Stanley Jefferson, the Indians leadoff man in the bottom of the first on Sunday. Jefferson's timing was terrible, since the Red Sox pitcher was Clemens. The Rocket Man threw a fastball that Jefferson took near the right elbow, and the benches emptied. Pena and Cleveland's Chris James were both ejected. Clemens was not and pitched the Sox to an 8-2 victory. In the aftermath, Morgan was asked if Clemens had thrown at Jefferson on purpose and was honest, as always. Sure, he said, adding, "We got even, didn't we? We had a silent vote on it the night before, and the vote was 24-0 in favor."

Poor Jefferson. The Sox had originally planned to drill Cleveland catcher Sandy Alomar Jr., but Alomar did not play, so Clemens figured he'd get it over with quickly. Jefferson was at least grateful that Clemens hadn't aimed at his head, but didn't sound exactly like Rambo when he said, "But he didn't have to throw it so hard."

Starting with that game, Boston went 19-6 over its next 25 to establish a 3 ½ game lead in the AL East. Morgan wasn't around for all of those games, though. His reward for being honest about throwing at Jefferson was a three-game suspension.

The Sox maintained their lead in the division as the season progressed in often illogical fashion. They had no speed and no power but found ways to win.

On July 17, both Brunansky and Jody Reed grounded into 5-4-3 triple plays in a game against the Twins at Fenway Park. As of 2005, it was still the only time in major league history a team hit into two triple plays in the same game. And the Sox won that game, 1-0. The night after that, still playing the Twins, Boston batters grounded into six double plays. And won that game, 5-4.

In late August, the Sox went to Toronto for a four-game series, holding a two-game lead over the Blue Jays. The Jays won the opener to make it a one-game deficit, then did not score another run. Boston won the next three games by scores of 2-0, 1-0 and 1-0 in a remarkable display of clutch pitching. The starters in those games were shopworn rookie Dana Kiecker, Clemens and converted reliever Greg Harris. Clemens pitched a complete game; unheralded rookie reliever Jeff Gray saved the other two.

On August 27 in Cleveland, the Sox won 12-4 and Ellis Burks hit two home runs in the fourth inning. He also admitted he thought that they came in different innings.

As September arrived, Boston was in command of the AL East. September, though, has never been a Red Sox fan's favorite month. It is when autumn arrives, and the fate of Boston teams in autumn is likely where the season got its nickname of "fall." September, 1990, started out like a lot of others.

It started with a new pitcher, Larry Andersen, a reliever brought in from the Astros to replace Reardon, who had had back surgery and was not expected to come back. Houston needed a third baseman, and the Sox had Boggs in the majors, Scott Cooper at Triple A and Jeff Bagwell at Double A. The Astros took Bagwell in what turned out to be one of the most awful trades in Red Sox history. Through the years, the Sox have liked to say that nobody could have projected Bagwell as a future MVP, but at the time of the deal, Morgan admitted, "The price was steep . . . Bagwell is a fine player."

For his part, Andersen stayed for the rest of the season, pitched OK, then left as a free agent, and Reardon made an historic return from what should have been season-ending surgery.

In Andersen, Boston got someone with the reputation as being one of those good guys in the clubhouse, a jokester who kept his teammates loose. Andersen was merely juvenile. His idea of funny was repetitive belching, each one an attempt to register on the Richter Scale, and while he eventually realized that all anyone was doing was rolling their eyes at him, for the first couple of weeks Andersen was on the roster, the Boston clubhouse sounded like Barnstable Harbor in the fog.

Which is how the Red Sox were playing. Reardon returned, but just as he did, Clemens went on the DL with a sore shoulder. Boston's first-place lead, once seven games, shrunk in a span of 15 days and disappeared completely on a mid-September road trip. On September 18, the Sox lost in Baltimore, 4-1, to fall into a first-place tie with the Blue Jays.

After the game, Pena blew up. He threw chairs around the clubhouse and filled the air with profanity, asking his teammates directly if they were quitters. After Pena dressed, Greenwell grabbed a chair of his own and threw it against Pena's locker. The next night, however, Boston lost again, this time 8-4. It was a galling defeat, since the winning pitcher was Curt Schilling, whom the Sox had traded away in 1988. The winning hit was a three-run homer by Sam Horn off of Harris who, after the game, said, "I feel like a [foolish] stupid idiot to let Sam Horn beat me in a game that means as much as this. It's ridiculous . . . no way I should be beaten by this man. That's the guy I wanted to pitch to, who's never touched me."

With their fans trembling at the thought of a late-season fold, like the ones in 1948, 1949, 1972, 1974, 1977 and 1978, the Sox regrouped. They battled for first with the Jays on a night-by-night basis, then Toronto arrived at Fenway for a three-game series. When it started, the teams were tied for first. In the first game, the Jays took a 6-5 lead into the last of the ninth, then the Red Sox tied it on Mike Greenwell's single off of Tom Henke. With the bases loaded and one out in a 6-6 game, Morgan let roster-filler Jeff Stone hit.

Stone was a late-season callup to pinch-run. He was a bit of base-ball legend, surrounded by stories such as the time he went out to dinner and declined a shrimp cocktail because he did not drink, or the time he left a TV in his Carribean apartment because it only got the Spanish channel.

Stone, in his first at-bat of the season, singled to right off of Henke and Boston was in first place to stay. Said Stone of his game-winning hit, "I'm on Cloud Ten."

The Sox clinched first place on the last day of the season, barely beating the White Sox, 3-1,when Brunansky went sliding into the right-field corner to make a sensational grab of what could have been a game-tying hit by Ozzie Guillen.

The playoffs were over quickly, though, as the Athletics ripped through the Sox in four straight, Boston scoring just four runs. In Game 4 in Oakland, Clemens was thrown out by plate umpire Terry Cooney after an argument in the second inning. While Sox fans could not fathom an ump throwing their ace out of a playoff game, Mike Gallego, who was the Oakland batter at the time and later went to spring training with the Sox, said that not only was Cooney justified in ejecting Clemens—he probably let him get away with more than he should have.

In the aftermath of the Oakland meltdown, Gorman purged the roster; finally, Boston's farm system, for years a cornucopia of young talent, was depleted, so the general manager made a disastrous foray into the free agent market.

Between the final playoff game in 1990, and opening day in 1991, the Red Sox either released or lost to free agency: Evans, Boddicker, Andersen, Barrett and Gardner. They signed Matt Young for two years at $5 million, Jack Clark for two years at $6 million and Danny Darwin for four years at $12 million.

It was an enormous waste of money.

Young was a very bright guy, a big left-hander with possibly the best pure arm in the league aside from Clemens. Young had positively terrifying stuff, and an equally terrifying lack of control, and during his years with the Mariners had pitched some terrific games against the Red Sox.

But it was a huge mistake bringing him from the relative anonymity of Seattle to the magnifying glass of Boston. Young did not handle the stress well, and by the end of his unhappy tenure with the Sox was so discombobulated emotionally that he couldn't bring himself to make throws to the bases, either to hold runners close, or to throw them out on grounders. In 1992, he had six errors in 16 fielding chances.

When things starting going badly, which was immediately, the Sox would have someone put the radar gun to Young when he was doing his pre-game warm-ups in the bullpen. They would compare those readings with his actual game performances, and find he consistently was five miles per hour or less during the games—that's how much the pressure of competition affected him.

Clark had somehow earned a reputation as a leader, but the Red Sox were his fifth team in the last eight years. He had hit some big home runs during his career, but in Boston he was a fraud. Clark hit a grand slam on opening day in 1991 to give the Sox a 6-2 victory in Toronto, but gave the Sox little besides headaches after that. It came as no surprise when he—despite becoming a millionaire thanks to baseball—went broke. After all, Clark used to give clubhouse boys one hundred dollar bills—and keep the change—to get him a hot dog out under the stands.

Darwin tried hard to earn his money and was a fierce competitor, but had never been more than a .500 pitcher and was just that with the Sox. He was probably best remembered for achieving a statistical impossibility in a game in Toronto on June 14, 1992.

He entered the game in the sixth inning in relief of starter Mike Gardiner. The bases were loaded, and Blue Jays catcher Kelly Gruber was ahead in the count, 2 balls and 0 strikes. Darwin threw two more balls to walk Gruber and force in a run, but according to the rules, the walk was charged to Gardiner. The next batter, John Olerud, hit a bases-clearing double, with all of the runs being charged to Gardiner.

That meant that Darwin had allowed four inherited runners to score.

Despite the reworked roster, or perhaps because of it, Boston started off pretty well in 1991 and as late as June 22 was in a first-place tie with the Blue Jays. It was an uneasy tie for first, though. A week earlier, Clark had caused his first problem of the season by telling San Francisco columnist Glenn Dickey that he wanted to be traded. Clark denied having said it, but he did say it, and Boston writers had already discovered that Clark tended to spout off without really thinking most of the time.

On June 2, the Sox once again extended Morgan's contract, this time through the end of 1992. Later that summer, in Texas, the writers who traveled regularly with Morgan and the Red Sox decided to belatedly take the manager out to lunch. They went to Coulter's, a barbecue joint not far from the old ballpark in Arlington, and in the middle of the meal, Morgan piped up with a question out of nowhere, asking, "So, how many of you guys here have ever smoked marijuana?"

A couple of hands went up, he acknowledged them, and got back to his barbecued chicken.

It was interesting that Morgan asked that particular question in that particular city, since it was in Arlington's old ballpark—a minor-league stadium that had been upgraded only slightly—that one Sox regular, being out of the lineup one night, slipped away from the dugout and could not be found when it was time for him to pinch-hit.

When he was found, it was in an aluminum groundskeepers shed under the third base grandstand, and he was indeed, smoking marijuana.

In the weeks after June 22, Boston went into one of its worst nose-dives ever. The Sox went 14-27 in their next 41 games, and lost 15 of 20 in a sickening three-week plunge at the end. As the losing continued, veteran slugger Mike Marshall languished on the bench, seeing little playing time for a manager who had little use for him.

In mid-July, the Red Sox were playing in Chicago, and Marshall decided to try the father-son approach with Morgan. During batting practice, Marshall sat down next to Morgan in the Boston dugout and said, "Joe, I'm at a crossroads here. I think I can help the ball-club. I want to help the ballclub. I'm ready to help the ballclub, but I'm not playing. If you were in my shoes, what would you do?"

Morgan never even glanced in Marshall's direction and answered, "I'd quit."

The Sox released him before the week was over.

On July 30, in the midst of the nosedive, reliever Jeff Gray suffered a stroke in the Sox clubhouse at Fenway Park before a game with the Rangers.

Gray had had a similar, but not as serious, incident when he was playing college baseball at Florida State. This time, the clubhouse was closed to the press as soon as Gray fell ill; players and coaches who remained inside said that watching the pitcher suffer was one of the most awful experiences of their lives.

Gray was an interesting player, and person. He had been signed as a free agent after being released by the Phillies in 1990 and had been called up to Boston midway through that season. Gray almost immediately became the team's best relief pitcher. Working in a setup role, he would come into tight games with runners all over the bases and work his way out of them thanks to an unhittable forkball.

He was obsessively meticulous. His roommates told stories of closets full of hangers all pointing in the same direction, of suitcases full of socks and underwear rolled into tight little balls and all stacked in neat rows. That obsession with order was apparent on the mound, as well. Gray took forever between pitches, making sure that everything was perfectly right before throwing the ball.

He was part pitcher, part scientist. Every pitch that Gray threw had a purpose, a plan, a direction. No pitcher on the Boston staff was more willing to talk about the science of pitching than Gray, and nobody understood the art form more than he did.

Gray recovered from the stroke and tried to pitch his way back to the majors, but could not make it back all the way. The Sox kept him around for a few years as a minor league pitching coach before he finally severed ties with the organization.

About a week after Gray's stroke the Red Sox—having endured a 5-15 stretch—had an off-day after being swept in Kansas City and headed into Toronto to face the first-place Blue Jays, who led the third-place Sox by 11 games.

The modern baseball manager is hired so someone can take the fall when players fail or general managers make bad decisions. Managers know that. They get paid pretty well for the privilege of being blamed for somebody else's mistakes and have their bank accounts to console them when they are finally let go.

What happened in August of 1991 calls into question the wisdom of firing managers, not that it will change things, but the 1991 Sox were going as badly then—worse even—than the 1988 team was going when McNamara was fired and Morgan replaced him.

But in 1991, Boston did not fire its manager, and the team went into Toronto and swept the Blue Jays. That unexpected, unlikely, illogical sweep turned the entire season around. Morgan's Magic? The 1991 Red Sox did not win 12 in a row, but were 31-10 in a span of 41 games. Over a longer period of time, they had a better record and made up more ground in the standings than the 1988 Sox did.

The surge threatened to be detoured in late August when Boston went to the West Coast. The Sox opened the road trip in Anaheim, and on August 24, as Boston's hitters took part in what seemed to be a routine batting practice, a fight broke out between Mo Vaughn and Mike Greenwell. It was later termed the "Rage in the Cage." The two men battled briefly, then were separated by Clark and third base coach Dick Berardino. Greenwell walked away with bruises on his face, marks which he made a point of insisting were caused by a bat.

Both men were adamant that the fight was not racially motivated. Greenwell said that Vaughn, a rookie, was needling him and took it beyond where a rookie should go. Before the game the next day, Morgan called the players into his office to meet and straighten things out and, after finishing with them, headed down to the field.

As he got into the dugout, a player came over and said, "Joe— what are you going to do about that?" and pointed to a man standing in the box seats at field level. The man had a sign which said that, when he had been a bat boy for the Sox some years ago, he had been molested by Boston equipment manager Don Fitzpatrick, who was in Anaheim with the team.

The players had all noticed the man with the sign and wanted Morgan to take some action. He didn't have the power to fire Fitzpatrick, so he simply had the equipment manager disengage himself from his duties. The disengagement turned out to be permanent, and Fitzpatrick officially resigned in early September.

Despite the ongoing turmoil, Boston almost caught Toronto thanks to more eclectic managing by Morgan. On September 13 in New York, the Sox trailed the Yankees in the sixth, 3-2. Boston had two men on against New York southpaw Jeff Johnson and Scott Cooper, a left-handed batter, was due up. Morgan pinch-hit for Cooper, but sent another lefty, Phil Plantier up, instead of a right-handed hitter.

Plantier's three-run homer put the Sox up, 5-3, and they won.

A 12-1 victory over the Yankees at Fenway on September 21 moved Boston to within a half-game of first. The next day, the Sox led, 5-4, with nobody on and two out in the top of the ninth when Reardon tried to throw an 0-2 fastball past Roberto Kelly.

Kelly hit it into the screen to make it 5-5. New York won in extra innings against Young and the season quickly unraveled. Boston went 3-10 the rest of the way and finished seven games out. The ending was unusually ugly, with players begging out of the lineup and sniping at each other and the manager, whom they had a hard time understanding. Of course they did. When it came to baseball, Morgan was so much smarter than them that they thought he was stupid.

The last game was at Fenway on October 6. Before the game, Morgan signed a lineup card for Steve Fainaru of the *Boston Globe*, inscribing on it, "The last go-round wasn't the best." It was more of Morgan's ESP at work, although he didn't know it at the time.

# SNAPSHOT

## The Definition of Pitching

As pure short-term fixes go, the trade that Lou Gorman made with the Reds after the 1988 season—Jeff Sellers and Todd Benzinger for Nick Esasky and Rob Murphy—was one of his best ever.

Esasky was the Sox' Most Valuable Player in 1989 before choosing to go to Atlanta via free agency. Murphy had a great year in 1989 before wearing down in 1990. For both of those two seasons, though, Murphy provided plenty to write about.

He was a combination of intellect and competitiveness, probably the first major league player to bring a laptop computer to the clubhouse on a regular basis. For Murphy, baseball was just one of his interests, and probably not the main one. He had developed a computer program to track the breeding of thoroughbred race horses and could, by assembling enough information about a thoroughbred's ancestry, make a reasonable prediction on how successful it would be as a racehorse.

Murphy also gave me the single most insightful quote I have ever gotten from a baseball player.

He was closing out a game against the White Sox on July 31, 1990 at Fenway and things were not going that well. Murphy had gotten two out, but had two men on base and went to a 3-2 count on the batter, Carlos Martinez. He threw a changeup about eye-high, and a foot outside. Martinez swung and missed for Strike Three and the game was over, Boston winning, 7-2.

Afterwards, I asked him, "So, you got Martinez to swing at Ball Four."

Murphy replied, "No. I got Martinez to swing at the illusion of Strike Three."

It was, essentially, the Encylopedia of Pitching in 11 words.

When Murphy pitched poorly, though, his temper got the best of him. He often would throw his glove into the stands after a bad performance. The fan who retrieved the glove would be a good Samaritan and try to return it, but Murphy usually didn't want it back.

In Kansas City on July 20, 1990 Murphy was belted around for three runs in just two thirds of an inning. After being relieved, he walked into the clubhouse and took his anger out on a table full of snack food. Teammate Dana Kiecker was sitting in front of his locker, facing away from Murphy, when a banana hit him in the back at high speed. Kiecker at first thought he had been speared with a javelin.

On August 15, 1990, in Oakland, Joe Morgan brought Murphy, a left-hander, in to face right-handed hitting Mark McGwire in the 10th inning of a 2-2 game. The A's had the bases loaded and nobody out. McGwire hit Murphy's first pitch off of the facing of the second deck in left field.

"I could have walked him, but it would have taken longer," said Boston's southpaw philosopher.

The 1989 season, in which he made 74 appearances and pitched 105 innings, took the zing out of Murphy's fastball and the Sox traded him just before the start of the 1991 season. He bounced around, and then went into his thoroughbred consulting business full-time.

Predictably, he flourished.

# The Firing of Joe Morgan

MOST RED SOX FANS OF A CERTAIN AGE REMEMBER WHERE THEY were and what they were doing on October 8, 1991, when they heard that Joe Morgan had been fired.

I was putting a new roof on my old garage when my wife hollered the news out the back door, and without bothering to call my editor, I showered, dressed and headed to Walpole, where Morgan lived in the same house he originally bought in 1955.

Departures of Red Sox managers are frequent and rarely lamented. Morgan had been the 23rd full-time manager since Ed Barrow led Boston to a World Series victory in 1918 and almost without exception, the public reaction to a firing was two words: Good riddance.

Morgan had been different, though. For one thing, he was a native New Englander, the first to manage the Red Sox since Charlestown's Shano Collins in 1931. Morgan's predecessor was the Nixonian John McNamara, who had been detested ever since he found a way to make all of the wrong moves in the closing games of the 1986 World Series.

Beyond that, Morgan was a refreshing change from the light-lipped, inarticulate, tobacco-chewing members of baseball's Old Boy

Network who generally controlled the game's dugouts. Morgan told the truth and knew how to use the language. He was funny and never took himself too seriously. Beyond that, he had the homespun sincerity and self-deprecation that the rest of the world imagined was inherent in every native New Englander.

Two stories illustrated Morgan's unique appeal.

One March day in 1990 in Winter Haven, Florida, where the Red Sox were holding spring training, a couple of fans called Morgan over to the box seats hoping for an autograph. They got much more than that. Morgan loved New England, and New Englanders, and never tired of finding out about them. He also had an uncanny knack for dialect. Talk to him long enough and he could probably nail down what part of New England you were from—Lynn as opposed to Cohasset, Worcester as opposed to Lowell.

He asked where these folks were from and found out that they lived in the Connecticut River Valley farming town of Montague. The farmer's name was Stan Smiarowski and he grew potatoes. Morgan had hit the jackpot, since he was a fanatical gardener and had stumbled upon a professional.

The Smiarowskis and Morgan talked for a while and he took their name, address and phone number and promised to call them when the season ended so he could drive out to the farm and look around. Fat chance of that, the Smiarowskis thought, but it had been very nice talking to the manager of the Red Sox.

So they were very surprised that fall when, after he had managed his team to the AL East title, Morgan indeed called and drove out for the first of what became annual visits to the Smiarowski farm in Montague.

One of the perks of being manager was that Morgan and his wife, Dorothy, got to go on the annual Red Sox cruise. One year on that cruise, the Morgans became friendly with a couple from Lunenburg, Massachusetts by the last name of Smith, or something like that. They said that they would be in Sarasota during spring training, so

Morgan told them to come to a Red Sox-White Sox game and look him up when they did.

The Sox versus Sox game in Sarasota that spring went on forever and Morgan and his players couldn't wait to get onto the bus and head back to Winter Haven. As he walked past the stands, Morgan heard someone calling his name and just gave a wave and got into his seat. As the bus drove away, it dawned on him who that fan was— the guy from Lunenburg.

He felt awful, but couldn't turn the bus around and try to track his friend down. Morgan stewed about what happened for the entire season. When it ended, he went to the cruise line and tracked down the names of the couple he thought he had snubbed in Sarasota. One winter day, Morgan drove out to the Lunenburg town hall, asked some suspicious town employees about the people he wanted to find, and was finally directed to how to get in touch with them.

There were a hundred stories like that, which is why New England let out a collective gasp when he was let go on that October day in 1991.

That morning, Morgan had headed into Fenway Park for what he thought was a discussion about the future of his coaching staff. Hitting coach Richie Hebner had come under fire from some players, anonymously of course, for his teaching methods. He was one of the greatest high school hockey players in the history of Massachusetts and, like most hockey people, was outspoken, blunt and candid.

Hebner was not one to pat a player on the behind and say "Nice job" when that wasn't true. One time, a player had stayed late to take lots of extra batting practice and still was having trouble getting his swing back. He asked Hebner if he had any advice and the hitting coach said, "Yeah—go home and play with your kids."

As Morgan drove up Route 1A towards Boston that morning, he figured he was going to be told to let Hebner, a friend, go. But when he arrived at Fenway and opened the door to the conference room, there sat the decision-makers in the Red Sox administration—co-owner Haywood Sullivan, general manager Lou Gorman and counsel John Donovan—with Jean Yawkey conspicuously absent.

Using one of his favorite terms, Morgan once described the scene by saying, "I smelled a rat."

The meeting began with the men in suits and ties fumbling for words like three actors auditioning to play the part of Ralph Kramden in the "Chef of the Future" skit. Finally, Morgan asked in general, "Am I in, or am I out?" And Sullivan replied, "Joe—you're out of there."

With that, Morgan got up from his seat, said "See you later, gents," and headed home.

With her husband gone to the ballpark, Dorothy Morgan had taken the morning to go shopping. She was in her car with the radio on when she heard that the Red Sox had scheduled a press conference for the afternoon. Having been around baseball since her marriage, Dot Morgan instinctively knew that Joe had been fired and cut short the shopping trip to get home.

I am from the Blackstone Valley town of Whitinsville, and Morgan had played in the Blackstone Valley League in the early 1950s, so we had become friends through talking about mutual acquaintances. On the day he was fired, I was able to drive right to his house on a residential side street in Walpole. When I arrived, the street was jammed with cars and television trucks and a score of reporters wandered around trying to find the former manager.

Only one had, Channel 4's Bob Neumeier. He got a poignant interview with Morgan, who had his grandson Anthony sitting on his lap as he talked with Neumeier. The interview ended with Morgan looking at his grandson and saying, "Anthony, your grampa got fired today" then adding some philosophical rumblings about how life goes on.

After that, Morgan and his wife hopped in their car and headed out of town to avoid the crush. Now, everybody with a tape recorder and notebook wanted to know where they had gone, but nobody in the Morgan house was saying. Bill Morgan, one of the four Morgan children, met me at the door and said, "All I can tell you is that they went far away. Down the Cape . . . way down the Cape."

While Cape Cod is generally considered to start at the Bourne and Sagamore Bridges, a sizeable part of the citizenry thinks that there is more to it than that. For them, Plymouth is the Cape. So is Mattapoisett. I wasn't aware of any friends Morgan had on Cape Cod, but was aware that Sox radio announcer Joe Castiglione lived in the South Shore town of Marshfield, and that the Morgans were very close friends with Joe Castiglione and his wife, Jan.

I found a pay phone along Route 1A and called the Castigliones. Jan Castiglione answered the phone and I asked her if the Morgans were there. She said they were not and that seemed to be that, since Jan Castiglione might say she couldn't tell me, but would never have lied.

Still, the day was early enough and I had nothing to lose, so I drove down to Marshfield and got there a bit after dark. The Marshfield police were very helpful in directing me to the address I had for the Castigliones. Their street was dark and the numbers on the houses were not visible from the road, so I stopped at what seemed like a friendly place and asked where the Castigliones lived. It was two houses down.

Jan Castiglione answered the door and said, "You're the only one I'd let in. And you know, when you called, they weren't here yet. I didn't lie."

The Morgans were in the family room, watching the Twins beat the Blue Jays in Game One of the ALCS on TV. Joe liked good scotch, and sipped on some as he looked dispassionately at the television. As he did, Jan walked out of the kitchen with some freshly baked brownies, and as he reflected upon his dismissal, the newest former manager of the Red Sox did it over the unlikely feast of Scotch and brownies.

Morgan's firing was big news around baseball. When Pirates manager Jim Leyland heard about it he said, "Joe Morgan fired? That means none of us are safe." The broadcast of the ALCS was constantly detouring to audio clips of Red Sox players reacting to Morgan's release, and none of the comments were very complimentary.

On came Jack Clark, Boston's aged Designated Hitter, and he was particularly critical of Morgan. Dot Morgan was infuriated and began to tell Clark stories, insisting that they be used in the newspaper and turned to her husband and said, "Joe—doesn't that make you mad?" And he replied in a measured tone, very calmly, rationally saying, "You have to remember something. Jack Clark has the mind of a 14-year-old."

Morgan spoke of veteran outfielder Tom Brunansky refusing to shake his hand when he arrived in the dugout after hitting a late-season home run and of some of the behind-the-scenes indignities every Red Sox manager had to deal with on a team where ownership had traditionally pampered its players.

Still, his firing and the subsequent hiring of Butch Hobson remain one of the great unsolved mysteries of the Yawkey years. That Jean Yawkey was behind it seems to be the most prevalent theory. Morgan had thought he was going to be fired in early August when his team hit a hideous skid, losing 15 of 20 games from July 18 through August 7, at one point falling 11 ½ games out of first place.

The end of that slump came in Kansas City, where the Sox lost consecutive shutouts to the Royals, then flew on Toronto. On the flight, Morgan confided in third base coach Dick Berardino that he expected to be fired any day now. The loyal Berardino told him not to worry, that Boston always played well in Toronto and would turn it around up there, but he was really just trying to make his boss feel better.

Berardino turned out to be a prophet. On August 9, in the first game of a four-game series, the Red Sox hammered David Wells and won 12-7. They wound up sweeping the Blue Jays, scoring 39 runs in the four games. That series set the stage for a Boston surge that was actually more impressive than Morgan's Magic in 1988, if not quite as starkly dramatic. The Sox went 31-9 over a 40-game stretch and eventually got to within a half-game of first place before fading.

Careful observers, though, could see signs that ownership was just looking for a reason to change managers. At a late-season charity function, Pawtucket Red Sox manager Butch Hobson was an invited guest and sat next to Jean Yawkey, who seemed completely taken with his southern charm. In contrast, she ignored Dot Morgan, to whom she had always been very friendly.

The Red Sox finished the 1991 season by losing nine of their last eleven games. The final game of the Morgan era was a 6-3 loss to the Brewers at Fenway Park on October 6, Roger Clemens, ever the warrior, throwing a complete game even though it was a meaningless one.

The day after he was fired, Morgan held a press conference at Fenway Park and talked about his dismissal, and his years with the Red Sox. For all of his managerial quirks, Morgan was an impeccable evaluator of talent and that was ultimately why his teams won so many games. And in that final press conference, he closed with a comment that served as a frighteningly accurate harbinger of what lay ahead in the Butch Hobson days.

"This team," Morgan said, "isn't as good as they think it is."

Morgan's 1991 Red Sox were 84-77. Boston would not break the .500 mark again until 1995.

# The Hobson Depression
## 1992 to 1994

ONE AFTERNOON IN THE SUMMER OF 1991, I VISITED MCCOY Stadium, and Pawtucket Red Sox general manager Mike Tamburro was on the field before a game and talking about the prospects down there. As usual, there were a few, but on this evening Tamburro went outside of the envelope a bit.

He pointed to the dugout where manager Butch Hobson and pitching coach Rich Gale were in a discussion and said, "There's the future of the Boston Red Sox."

Tamburro, who loved Joe Morgan, had no idea of how prescient he was. No sooner had the Morgan firing been announced than Hobson was introduced as his replacement. It seemed like a logical move, and Hobson had indeed gotten a reputation in the minor leagues as sort of a "new wave" manager although, in the medieval culture that had become the Red Sox farm system, being modern was a relative term.

Hobson and Gale came to Boston as a package deal. Hobson had been a very popular Red Sox player, and even after his skills had been diminished by injuries, was a respected teammate and opponent for his selfless competitive spirit. The assumption was that he would bring that to Fenway Park.

Hobson did not change the Red Sox culture, however. It changed him, and it did not take long.

The spring of 1992 was a year in which Roger Clemens chose to send a message by reporting to training camp late. His belated arrival was eagerly anticipated; when Hobson was a player, he would have swum through the Everglades to be on time for training camp. The meeting of veteran pitcher and rookie manager was expected to be explosive.

Instead, on Clemens' first day at camp, Hobson joined him in a pleasant jog. He had not managed his first regular-season game yet and already the new manager looked more like Billy Herman than Billy Martin.

And that never changed.

The Hobson years, which spanned 1992 through the premature end of the 1994 season, were the dreariest along Yawkey Way since the Impossible Dream revived the catatonic franchise in 1967. The Sox finished below .500 for three straight seasons for the first time since a stretch from 1959 to 1966. Under Hobson, Boston played baseball in waves—the Red Sox would surge into contention on hot streaks, then fall off in longer, colder, slumps.

In 1993, for instance, Boston was eight games under .500 and 13 games out of first place on June 20. The Sox went 25-8 after that and were tied for first on July 25, but were 19-35 down the stretch and finished below .500. In 1994 they started out 26-13 and were 54-61 when the year was finally foreclosed on by a strike.

Hobson's term as Boston manager was marked mostly by a series of odd, usually disconnected, sideshows, and the performances began on Opening Day in 1992. The Sox lost that game in Yankee Stadium with Clemens pitching only moderately well. It turned out that before the game, while stretching in the dugout, the Rocket Man had somehow smashed his right pinky finger into the concrete ceiling of the Boston dugout.

In Clemensese, he said he "smoked his pinky." Clemens was

sent back to Boston to have the finger checked while the Sox, who went 0-2 in New York to open the season, went on to Cleveland and played the Indians in the Tribe's home opener on Saturday, April 11.

The stands at cavernous old Cleveland Stadium had some 65,000 fans in them, about 60,000 more than normal. The game started at 1:05 P.M. and ended after 7:30. The teams were tied, 5-5, after seven innings and the score stayed that way until the top of the 19th, when Tim Naehring hit a two-run homer to left. Boston held on to win, 7-5, and Hobson had his first victory as Red Sox manager.

But he had to use eight pitchers to do so, and the teams had a doubleheader scheduled for Sunday.

As Saturday's game droned on, Clemens was at his home in Framingham, doing wind sprints up and down his 400-yard long driveway, the kind of driveway only a man making $4,555,250 a year could afford to have paved. Clemens realized how spent the Boston pitching staff was, called the Sox clubhouse during Saturday's game, and told them he would fly into Cleveland on Sunday and pitch later that day. Fast forward the clock about ten years or so and try to imagine Pedro Martinez doing that.

The starter for the first game of that Sunday doubleheader was Matt Young, whose unfortunate reputation as some sort of left-handed banana republic was about to be enhanced. For, in that first game, Young accomplished one of the rarest feats possible in baseball, something just this side of hitting a five-run homer.

He pitched a no-hitter and lost, 2-1.

Young didn't allow a hit in his eight innings, but walked seven. Shortstop Luis Rivera made a throwing error in the first inning to allow Indians leadoff man Kenny Lofton to score. Young had walked Lofton, then let him steal second and third. Two more walks in the third led to another Cleveland run; Boston scored a run in the fourth and that was it. The Indians used three pitchers and the Red Sox outhit the Tribe, 9-0, but lost anyway.

After the game, Young was brought out from the Boston club-house and met with reporters in a tiny passageway just outside of the door. He talked about what he had just done, and how it happened, with the resignation of a man who had gotten a 59 on every test he had ever taken in his life. A year earlier, baseball commissioner Fay Vincent had ruled that no-hitters of less than nine innings would no longer be recognized as such, and Sean McAdam of the *Providence Journal* brought that up during the interview.

Finally, Young was asked when he knew that his effort that day was not going to be counted as a no-hitter. He nodded sadly towards McAdam and said, "Not until the Grim Reaper here told me." Later, in talking about his performance, Young said, "I would have pitched to them in the bottom of the ninth, but they didn't want to hit."

For the record, the Red Sox recognize Young's performance as a no-hitter and so does the Hall of Fame. How it can be considered a regulation complete game, but not a no-hitter, is beyond logic, but this is baseball, which at times seems to have been invented to refute logic.

As a sidelight to the Young game, his catcher was rookie John Flaherty, who made his major-league debut that day. Flaherty is the only man to catch a no-hitter in his first big league appearance.

Young had just about finished his post-game interview when the second game started, with Clemens on the mound for the Sox, smoked pinky and all. The Rocket Man pitched a 3-0 shutout, striking out 12 Indians, allowing two hits. On Saturday night, Cleveland got 20 hits in 19 innings and lost. On Sunday, the Indians got two hits in two games and split a doubleheader.

"What a country," Tribe manager Mike Hargrove said.

By the beginning of August, Boston was 13 1/2 games out of first place. On August 3, the Sox played the Blue Jays at Fenway Park and outfielder Billy Hatcher stole home in a 7-1 victory. It was a straight steal of home, the kind that Ty Cobb and Jackie Robinson had done, but the kind Red Sox players never did. Boston didn't have a sign for it, and after the game Hobson, in an Andy Griffith moment, said his reaction to Hatcher taking off was "[Fudge]. He's fixin' to steal home."

On August 30, Boston traded Jeff Reardon to the Braves for two minor leaguers. Reardon had helped the Sox win in 1990, but was another example of a guy that Boston had acquired too late in his career. Gruff, honest, a blue-collar pitcher from the blue-collar background of Dalton, Massachusetts, Reardon had lost his fastball and resorted to getting hitters out mostly on stubbornness, and that only went so far.

The end came in Anaheim, during the middle of a game against the Angels that Boston eventually won, 3-2. The disenchanted Reardon had already cleaned out his locker back at Fenway before the trip west started and could not wait to get out of the Sox club-house after the game ended. But his exit was delayed. As Reardon tried to get out the door, trainer Charlie Moss approached him holding two new baseballs. "Jeff, sign these before you go, please," said Moss, and a disgusted Reardon scribbled his name twice, turned and headed for the airport.

With players crossing the days off their calendars as September arrived, there were a couple of final pieces of messy business to transact, and they happened within a week of each other.

On September 12, the Sox lost to the Tigers at Fenway Park, 9-5. Clemens got the loss. Detroit led, 1-0, going into the fifth and Tony Phillips led off the inning with a ground ball that went past Boggs and into left field. It was ruled an error and Detroit eventually got two unearned runs out of it. After the game, Boggs went to official scorer Charles Scoggins and asked to have the call changed, from an error to a hit. Scoggins agreed and it cost Clemens two earned runs, lifting his ERA from 2.26 to 2.31 with him still a candidate for the Cy Young Award.

The change became common knowledge on September 15 and when reporters asked Clemens about it, he took the unusual step of asking them out into the players parking lot to discuss it. Many reporters had never ventured out into the players lot, a tiny piece of asphalt pie tucked into the corner of Yawkey Way and Van Ness Street. The players parking lot was like the dead line in the movie *The Great Escape*. Fenway security was thought to have "shoot to kill" orders for those venturing onto the pavement.

Out there, as we stood amongst the BMWs and Lincolns, Clemens calmly shredded his team's third baseman, saying that one reason Boggs' request hurt so much was that in 1987, when an injured Boggs was battling Paul Molitor for a batting title, Clemens took extra pride in getting Molitor out "while Wade was sitting on his average up in the clubhouse."

Boggs went into a tirade when asked about the play, saying, "Are we giving out errors because he's Roger Clemens? If it was an error, I'd say it was an error. I'm not trying to [hurt] anyone. Change it back." Boggs then suggested some unhygienic activities for those who cared to try them, and the interview was over.

On May 11, Mo Vaughn had been demoted to Pawtucket after a series of games in which he had looked terrible at the plate and had botched routine plays in the field. While he was eventually recalled, and eventually began to play like the MVP he would become, Vaughn was crushed by the demotion and things were never good again between him and Hobson.

On September 20, Boston was in Detroit and beat the Tigers in a Sunday afternoon game, 5-4, and after the game most of the players and coaches, and Hobson, went out to dinner at the 1940 Chop House downtown. Things went so well that some of the Sox party went to suburban Dearborn, where the team stayed, and continued the festivities at the Hyatt Hotel. Late in the night, however, things got ugly as Vaughn and Hobson got into an altercation.

"It wasn't a fight, exactly," said Phil Plantier, who saw it. "I'm not sure how to describe it. It was something out of the WWF [World Wrestling Federation] I guess."

It took a while to ferret out the story. I got the full details a few days later when the Sox were in Baltimore and wanted to get Vaughn alone to talk about it. One afternoon, I sat in the corridor outside of his hotel room at the Marriott, alone with a copy of the *Baltimore Sun* and surrounded by last night's room service leftovers, until Vaughn finally came out.

"What happened in Detroit between Hobson and you?" I asked him.

"Let it go, man," Vaughn replied. "Let it go. It's over. I'm not saying anything about it."

"I'm writing about it anyway," I said. "I won't if it didn't happen, but I have to know if it did."

"Let it go," Vaughn said for one last time. "I'm not saying it didn't happen, but let it go, please."

I didn't let it go. It was too good a story. Hobson denied it, but it happened. Both men worked together for the next two years without repercussions but were never especially close.

In 1993, Boston's roller-coaster season saw the Sox in first place in late July before going into a sickening fold. The beginning of the end of Boston being in contention coincided with a strange incident that, had it happened a dozen years later, would have been called "Roger being Roger."

The Red Sox were within 1 ½ games of first place on July 31 when Clemens lost a 4-0 shutout in Baltimore, on a Saturday night. At 6:30 the next morning, Clemens and some teammates—John Dopson for sure, and perhaps Scott Cooper—stopped on a highway leading into downtown to help a dog that had been hit by a car.

Clemens was bitten on the right thumb. Nobody questioned his kindness, but there was some concern about he and his teammates being out and about at 6:30 A.M., since they were coming back from dinner, not going to breakfast, and Boston had a game at 1:35 that afternoon.

Hobson's biggest concern was that his pitcher might have rabies, and imagine that on the Disabled List wire—Clemens, Boston, 15 days (rabies)—but tests proved negative. As for his players being out at 6:30 A.M., that was an in-house thing and was taken care of. As the team left Baltimore, Clemens tried to duck reporters by going out one of the clubhouse's side doors and hopping a golf cart, but he was discovered.

His last words, as he left a pack of reporters in the dust of the Camden Yards hallways, were "Bob Barker's got nothing on me."

By late September, Boston was hopelessly out of the pennant race. The Sox went on their final road trip of the season, four games in New York, then three in Toronto. The trip did nothing to help the Red Sox in the standings, but did a lot to add to their almost 80-year legacy of unfathomable public failure.

On the night of September 18 at Yankee Stadium, Boston had a 3-1 lead over New York with two out and nobody on base in the last of the ninth. Reliever Greg Harris hit Mike Gallego with a pitch, then he induced Mike Stanley to hit a soft fly ball to Mike Greenwell in left for the final out of the game.

Except.

As Harris threw that last pitch to Stanley, a teenager at the game with a church group jumped out of the stands and onto the field near third base. Third base umpire Tim Welke called time—before Harris delivered, he said—and after a long discussion, the play became a do-over. Stanley singled.

In quick order, Boggs—now with the Yankees—reached on an infield hit that scored Gallego. Dion James walked to load the bases, and Don Mattingly hit a two-run single to right field. Final score: Yankees 4, Red Sox 3. Boston protested, but filed it too late to have a hearing. Cooper, the third baseman, readily admitted that Welke had called time before the pitch was delivered. Hobson was furious, so much so that the next day he seriously suggested that New York police and stadium security be allowed to beat up trespassers on the field as an example to the rest of the crowd.

Vaughn, meanwhile, just rolled his eyes when asked about the game and said, "This [stuff] always happens to the Red Sox, nobody else. When they called time and we had to do it over, I knew we were in [deep stuff] right there."

The next day, Boston won a Sunday afternoon game, 8-3, and headed for Toronto. Traditionally, during the season's final road trip, Red Sox rookies were subjected to some sort of hazing. In 1992, they had their lockers emptied and were forced to board the team plane dressed as cartoon superheroes. This time, when the rookies returned to their lockers, they found their regular clothes gone and women's clothing in its place.

Veterans watched gleefully as the kids put on their new attire, none of it very fashionable. Pitcher Cory Bailey's outfit was too small. Pitcher Ken Ryan's was too big. Catcher Tony Pena looked at Bailey and said, "Why don't you try on Kenny's dress?"

In time, the team headed off to LaGuardia. Some fans were there and saw the Sox rookies dressed like girls, and Harrington read about the Animal House antics in the next day's papers. He was livid and called Hobson to express his opinion.

Hobson was affable and approachable as manager and rarely lost his temper. One time, *Globe* columnist Dan Shaughnessy told Hobson that he was going to write that the manager should be fired, and Hobson told Shaughnessy that's OK, you are welcome in my office any day. Hobson spoke Southern homespunese most of the time—"Good things happen to good people" was a favorite— and in general he was easy to deal with.

In Toronto, though, things were different. His ears still burning from the Harrington call, Hobson sat seething behind his desk in his tiny Skydome office as reporters filed in before that night's game. His eyes narrowed, Hobson recounted how Harrington had called him, how the owner had said it's just not right that members of the Boston Red Sox be seen in public dressed like women.

Hobson stood up from behind the desk and approached the group of silent reporters and hissed at them that it wasn't bad enough that they wrote about it—he had figured it would be off the record, although nobody had ever said that—but that they didn't even get it right.

"I was told," Hobson said icily, "that somebody wrote where they saw Cory Bailey wearing a dress. Cory Bailey wasn't wearing a [foolish] dress.

"It was a jumper.

"With a nice, blousy shirt.

"And cowboy boots."

End of pre-game press conference. The journalists, about half a dozen strong, filed silently out of the office, still trying to process what they had just been told by the manager of the Boston Red Sox, upset over the fact that the feminine attire on one of his pitchers had been misrepresented.

The initial reaction was that a) it was a joke; b) it was a dream; or c) they had heard something wrong. Finally, somebody giggled, and that put a quick end to any journalistic decorum. Boston was beaten that night, 5-0, in a game nobody saw much of. We all spent most of the evening trying to stifle laughter, and not doing too well at it.

Hobson had one more year left after 1993, but Gorman did not. He was replaced as general manager by Dan Duquette, and Duquette stuck with Hobson for 1994. He had nothing to lose. The 1994 Sox were not his team and who managed them was mostly irrelevant. Duquette spent most of 1994 planning for 1995 and dealing with the looming threat of a players' strike.

He did make several deals along the way, two of them simply awful, but in June he directed the first amateur draft of his tenure in Boston. Duquette's first pick ever was a shortstop from Georgia Tech, Nomar Garciaparra.

On April 1, Duquette traded catchers with the Tigers. Detroit got the light-hitting, but defensively strong Flaherty while Boston obtained the heavy-hitting, but defensively weak Rich Rowland. It was a bad omen as to the direction the team would take under Duquette.

Rowland became best known for two things. One was when he was the subject of a feature story by Nick Cafardo of the *Boston Globe*. In the course of interviewing people from Rowland's past, Cafardo discovered that the catcher was actually three full years older than he said—31, not 28. And in 1995, when he was demoted to Pawtucket, Rowland came to Fenway Park to get his equipment and found the clubhouse locked, so he took a baseball bat and smashed the door in.

Another horrible deal was made on May 31 when Duquette traded the indefatigable Paul Quantrill and Billy Hatcher to the Phillies for Wes Chamberlain. Chamberlain was sullen and surly, a one-dimensional righty hitter with occasional power. Both he and Rowland were gone for good by 1996, while Flaherty and Quantrill were both still in the major leagues in 2005.

The Red Sox dropped out of contention in early June, and as it was the year before, the drop was a vertical one. Boston was 30-18 on May 30, 40-43 on July 7.

Not long after the All-Star break, the Red Sox headed west for one of their biennial trips up and down the Pacific Coast. By now, Boston was running out of pitchers and Duquette called up Tim VanEgmond from Pawtucket. A quiet, pleasant young man born, raised and educated in the deep south, VanEgmond was one of Hobson's "Good things happen to good people" and flew into John Wayne Airport in Santa Ana on the evening of July 17. Many members of the media corps were landing at the same time, fresh in from Oakland where Boston had taken three games of a four-game series. As I got my bags from the carousel, WBZ radio correspondent Jonny Miller did, too. Miller had rented a car and, considerate as always, offered me a ride to the Anaheim Marriott.

That is where the team stayed, too, and when we saw

VanEgmond, Miller offered him a ride. The pitcher was glad to accept and we took our bags across the street to the garage where the rental cars were, hopped in, and headed for the Marriott with Miller behind the wheel.

Southern California traffic is bad under good conditions, and these were not good conditions. Interstate 5 was being rebuilt and it snaked past the strip malls, office parks and apartment complexes in a maze of Jersey barriers and wire fences. Not that this was of any concern to those driving. It was bumper-to-bumper, occasionally fender-to-fender, at 75 miles per hour.

Miller was a native New Englander and a little traffic did not intimidate him.

He barreled north on the interstate like everyone else, left-lane, right-lane, watch-where-you're-going, tires squealing, horns everywhere. There were no roads like this in Alabama, and as I leaned over to say something to VanEgmond in the back seat, I noticed his eyes getting wider and his breathing getting shallower. All of our luggage couldn't fit in the trunk, so some was in the back with VanEgmond. Before long, he had taken it and surrounded himself with ramparts of suitcases and spent the rest of the trip crouched behind them.

Miller did, of course, deliver everyone safely to the hotel. Unfailingly polite, VanEgmond disembarked from the car. Sweating profusely, he thanked Miller equally profusely for the ride, checked in, and went up to his room to contemplate his start the next day.

Now, pitchers have bad games, hairy car rides or not, so there is no way to prove any connection between the trip from the airport and what happened the next day.

Which was that Boston got two runs for VanEgmond in the top of the first; he then took the mound, faced nine Angels batters, gave up hits for the cycle—a single, double, triple and home run—and walked three as California scored nine runs.

The season ended in the rain in Baltimore on August 11. The Sox had lost an awful game to the Twins on the night before, 17-7 in Minneapolis, and got underway the next night before it started to pour. The game was called off and on the next day, the Players Association began a strike that eventually canceled the rest of the regular season and all of the post-season.

Everyone headed home that morning. Most players got out of town as quickly and inconspicuously as possible. Reliever Ken Ryan, from Seekonk, Massachusetts, had his parents in town with him and was in the lobby waiting for them to come down. Ryan was one of the finest gentlemen on the team and incapable of being rude, so when approached by reporters for comment on the strike, he provided them with the standard "We all just want to play base-ball" and sat back down on a couch.

"I'm not looking forward to this," Ryan said to a couple of us who had stuck around to converse. The strike, you mean, he was asked. "No, the ride home," he replied.

Ryan's father was a policeman who, over the years, had helped pull too many mangled bodies out of cars, and he drove like a Red Sox catcher running out a grounder to second. "How long a drive is it from here back home?" Ryan asked. "Six or seven hours," I told him.

"Make that nine or ten," he replied, "with my dad driving."

With that, the Ryans pulled up in front of the hotel and Ken got into the car, crouching down in the back seat like a 10-year-old boy being dragged to his first square dance lesson.

It would be a long time before Ryan threw another pitch, and when he did, almost nothing from 1994 would still be around.

# SNAPSHOT

## Tony Pena and the Haircut

By the summer of 1993, Tony Pena's career with the Red Sox was nearing an end. The veteran catcher's bat had slowed so much that he was almost treated like a pitcher in the Boston batting order. He would bunt whenever he came up with someone on base, and opposing teams would often walk the Sox' Number 8 hitter, usually rookie shortstop John Valentin, to pitch to Pena.

Nevertheless, Pena remained a vibrant, vocal presence on the roster—not just with his teammates, but with everyone around the club.

Which explains why on July 28 of that year, as I stood in line at the front desk of the Pfister Hotel in Milwaukee to get change for a $100 bill, Pena walked by and began scolding me over the increasing length of my gray hair.

"You need a haircut," he said. "Your hair is too long. Too gray. It has to go."

I explained that being on the road made it tough, since I only had my hair cut by my barber back home. That was not a good enough explanation for Pena, who replied, "I cut my kids' hair. I do a good job. Let me cut yours. No charge. C'mon, let's go. Let's do it now."

Pena was relentless and I finally weakened, fending him off with what seemed like a very reasonable proposition. I'd let him cut my hair if he hit a home run before I got home to the barber. In return, he would no longer make an issue of my hair.

At the time, Pena was batting .171 and had hit one home run in the previous 14 months.

Rookie John Flaherty caught the game that night in Milwaukee and Pena went according to form the next night, going a weak 0 for 3. The night of July 30 found the Sox in Baltimore, where the Orioles were in their second season at Camden Yards. Lefty Jamie Moyer was the Baltimore pitcher when Pena, batting ninth, came up with one out in the top of the second. Moyer threw Ball One, then Pena hit the next pitch to straightaway center field, where it carried over the fence and into the bullpens beyond. It was one of the longest balls Pena had ever hit as a Red Sox.

After the game, I went to the clubhouse and talked to manager Butch Hobson in his office and was able to avoid going into the main part of the clubhouse where the players dressed. But, the next afternoon there was no escaping Pena. I walked in at 3:30 sharp and he was ready.

He grabbed a chair from in front of his locker and went into the shower room to bring out some towels, which he then wrapped around my neck to catch the clippings. Using a pair of scissors borrowed from trainer Charlie Moss, who used them to cut adhesive tape, Pena went to work on my hair.

It was awful.

He snipped away and the hair fell off in uneven clumps. Shortstop Luis Rivera came over to watch and the men began talking excitedly in Spanish, and the more excited they got, the more hair wound up on the floor. As Pena cut, he chomped on a wad of tobacco, spitting the juice into an empty plastic bubble gum bucket on the floor.

Eventually, he dropped the tape scissors into the pail of juice. When he fished them out and prepared to keep cutting,

I got up and told him he had done enough. He agreed, unwrapped the towels from around my neck, and it was over.

It was a typical Baltimore July day and night, brutally hot and inhumanely sticky. The towels had not done a very good job of shielding my neck and it practically sizzled from the tiny bits of hair stuck between the skin and the collar of my shirt. The game, which Baltimore won, 4-0, took forever to play and as soon as I opened the door to my room, I jumped into the shower.

The very next day, the phone began ringing. Red Sox broadcaster Bob Montgomery had seen the haircut and talked about it on TV. *Sports Illustrated* called. So did radio station WEEI in Boston, and they had me on to explain what happened. In the aftermath, some 75 different barbers and hair stylists called to offer me a free fix—the haircut was beyond bad—but I waited to get home.

The women at Chick's in Whitinsville, where I got my hair cut then and still do, cut it short and made it look at least presentable until it grew back. For years afterwards, Pena would find me when whatever team he worked for came into Boston and mention that my hair seemed too long.

That was the last bet I ever made with a baseball player.

# The North Korea of Baseball

AROUND SUPPER TIME ON THE EVENING OF NOVEMBER 8, 1993, the phones rang at the homes of most of the writers who covered the Red Sox on a regular basis. The caller was Lou Gorman, and the news was that he would no longer be the general manager of the Sox.

This was typical of Gorman, whose years in the navy—which is where he met, and dated, movie star Kim Novak before settling down to get married—had instilled a very strong sense of duty in him. Gorman did things the right way, even when doing it the right way wasn't all that pleasant.

When he called me, I asked him, "Where will you find a replacement? Will you hire from within the organization?" To which Gorman replied, "I'm not sure if we'll look in-house, or out-house."

The Sox looked outhouse.

In January, they announced the hiring of Dan Duquette as the new general manager. A native of the Western Massachusetts town of Dalton, where the paper for the dollar bill was made, Duquette had been an excellent student and athlete at Wahconah Regional High, played varsity baseball and football at Amherst College, and had risen from the penny-ante paycheck ranks of baseball's front offices to become general manager of the Expos.

Duquette had been a good GM in Montreal, building strong teams without a lot of money to work with. As he came home to Boston, to his dream job running the Red Sox, the move seemed like a perfect fit.

Nobody seems to know what happened to Duquette from the time he took over as GM in January of 1994 until the day he was fired in spring training of 2002. But during those years, the Red Sox went from being one of baseball's most-respected organizations to one that perfected the concept of institutional arrogance.

Boston became the North Korea of baseball.

Some of it was John Harrington's fault. The Red Sox' defacto owner, even though his legal role was trustee, became less and less involved with the team as time went on. He became involved with league affairs, then in trying to get a new ballpark built, then, finally, in selling the franchise. Duquette filled the leadership vacuum and along the way, the Boston franchise was stripped of its humanity.

Duquette was general manager for eight seasons and in the course of those eight seasons, 238 different men played games in a Red Sox uniform. In comparison, that's almost the exact same number of different players employed by Boston during the 21 baseball seasons from 1973 through Gorman's last season in 1993.

He was never outgoing, but during Duquette's first couple of years as general manager, he was at least approachable and often funny in a very dry way. During his first year, 1994, Duquette was asked to take part in a seminar at the Boston Public Library. In a question-and-answer session after the seminar, a fan asked Duquette about Phil Plantier, a former Red Sox outfielder who had hit 34 homers for San Diego in 1993 after hitting seven for Boston in 1992. The rap on Plantier was that he had a bad attitude.

To which Duquette responded, "From seven homers to 34? His attitude got a lot better, didn't it?"

The 1994 season ended prematurely due to a players' strike, and the Sox were rained out in Baltimore on a night that would have been their final game. During the rain, and before the game was called, Duquette sat in the Camden Yards dining room and chatted with reporters. He was asked about Rich Rowland, the Boston catcher with huge muscles, a tiny batting average and substantial defensive problems.

"We're not sure what to do with Rowland," Duquette said. "He's spent so much time chasing passed balls he knows the season-ticket holders in the box seats better than our pitchers."

Duquette had traded to get Rowland, so his comment was not just funny, it was self-deprecating. But there was little of that in the future.

By the end of the 1996 season, Duquette had become mostly inaccessible to the news media. When he did answer questions, the responses were generally obtuse, often convoluted, and usually disconnected from the original topic. That winter, the team's regular writers asked Harrington if he would meet with them to try and reopen the lines of communication with the front office.

He did meet, on a very dreary December afternoon at Fenway Park, and the session was short. The writers told Harrington what their concerns were and suggested possible remedies. Harrington, with Duquette at his side, said simply, "Dan's my general manager. Whatever he thinks is the best way to do his job, I'll back him."

That was the end of the meeting, and the unofficial naming of Duquette as Emperor of Yawkey Way.

How players and managers and even general managers deal with the press is of little consequence, but Duquette's dealings with the news media were symptomatic of how he dealt with everybody, and that was the problem.

For instance, through the years, he did a pre-game radio spot with broadcaster Jerry Trupiano. When the Sox were on the road, Duquette would generally call Trupiano in the afternoon to tape the little interview and Trupiano would have to wait at the phone for the GM to call.

On too many occasions, Trupiano would sit in the radio booth doing nothing, just waiting for the phone to ring, Duquette having disregarded whatever time the men had set up previously.

Long-time Red Sox employees like Johnny Pesky and Sam Mele were made to feel unwelcome, and many former players got the same impression—that their contributions in the past meant nothing. One longtime Sox employee who had worked in the baseball end of the organization for years, confided in me that it had reached the point where he was ashamed to tell people he worked for the Red Sox, something he could never imagine having happened. The conversation ended by him saying, "I know we are the most disliked organization in baseball."

It's one thing for a general manager to not return reporters' calls, but Duquette got to the point where he wouldn't even return other general managers' calls. During the 2000 season, one AL general manager wanted to make a mid-level trade with the Sox and kept calling, but could not get through to Duquette. Instead, he kept getting referred to assistant general manager Lee Thomas, who said he'd check with Dan and get back to him.

Finally, the other GM got hold of Duquette, but by then, trading was not on his mind. The phone call was short, and went something like this:

"Don't ever call us again to talk about a trade. We don't want to deal with you any more. You have no clue how to treat people. Good bye."

Sox players despised Duquette, not that players everywhere don't have some animosity towards whoever the general manager might be, but this was beyond the normal "us against them" feelings.

In 1999, Duquette had roster problems and tried to force catcher Scott Hatteberg onto the Disabled List even though he wasn't hurt. Hatteberg was involved in union affairs and was nobody's pushover and fought the battle publicly, unlike some players who simply did what they were told even though they knew it was wrong. When veteran Mike Stanley, one of the most respected men in the game, was released in 2000, it was done through messages and intermediaries rather than face to face.

In 1994, Duquette acquired Stan Royer, a third baseman who once had shown some power for the Cardinals, played him for a couple of weeks, then sent him to Pawtucket. But Royer went home to St. Louis rather than the minors, so the Sox put him on the Disqualified List. And kept him there for years, as it turned out, just for spite.

I called Royer once to do a flashback sort of story and Royer, a successful financial advisor in St. Louis, was bewildered by how long he was on the Disqualified List. "Who did he think I was—Bo Jackson?" Royer wondered when asked about Duquette.

Popular infielder Lou Merloni never got to big-money levels with the Sox, and had not been in the majors long enough to qualify for arbitration at first, so he had to undergo an annual spring training battle for money. One year, he and Duquette threw around some figures and could not agree, so the Sox exercised their right to simply renew Merloni's contract. When they did, the figure was $50,000 less than the final offer they had made when negotiating. All Duquette neglected to do was provide Merloni with a jar of Vaseline.

Nobody had less regard for Duquette than Marty Cordova, an outfielder who Duquette invited to spring training in 2000. Cordova was Duquette's type of player, a big, strong slugger who might benefit from a change in scenery. A few other teams were also interested in Cordova, but Duquette's pursuit was relentless. The GM would call Cordova from a ski slope in Quebec trying to convince him to come to Boston, although he could not promise him a spot on the 40-man roster, so could only offer him a provisional contract.

Finally, Cordova cracked. He told Duquette, "OK, I want to come to Boston. You guys have a chance to win, and I'll take the deal, but you have to promise me you're sincere about keeping me because I can get more money guaranteed someplace else."

Duquette said he meant it, so Cordova signed. A month into spring training of 2000, he was released and eventually picked up by Toronto. "Why do that to me?" asked an infuriated Cordova. "It cost me a million dollars. Now, I know I've already made some money in this game, but nobody likes to lose a million dollars no matter how much you've made."

The lowest point of the Duquette years, though, happened at the end of the 2000 season. In September, Carl Everett and manager Jimy Williams were at odds, and eventually Duquette and Williams as well, so the GM agreed to meet with reporters to discuss the ongoing turmoil. It was a waste of time, of course, with Duquette responding to questions with vague answers and eventually, it got to be too much for veteran radio reporter Jon Miller.

Miller, who had covered the team for WBZ since box seats cost $3, lambasted Duquette with an outburst that began, "I'm sick of your doubletalk." Things eventually calmed down and everybody went back to work, knowing no more than before the press conference, but the depth of the Sox' pettiness and vindictiveness was endless.

To retaliate against Miller, they refused to issue him a season credential for 2001. This meant that he had to re-apply for media passes, generally for each series, adding a whole new layer of aggravation to the job of following the Red Sox, since he also traveled to their road games. It was common, during the summer of 2001, to walk into the ballpark before a Sox road game and find Miller waiting at the door for someone to bring down his pass so he could go in and start working.

As Harrington became less and less involved in actually running the team, the Red Sox became more and more like a Warsaw Pact nation. The organization had become a sycophantocracy, where loyalty to Duquette meant more than ability.

Even the players understood this. Matt Stairs was one of Duquette's first acquisitions, but never played very much in Boston.

He eventually went on to fashion an excellent big-league career as a dangerous left-handed hitter. Asked about Duquette during the summer of 1998, Stairs replied, "I should be thankful to him for letting me leave. Anybody who's not his boy has to leave."

The turnover in the player development system and front office was breathtaking. It became a running joke to those who kept track of such things. Who was in and who was out was like the old May Day parade in Moscow. The closer you stood to Brezhnev, the brighter your future.

At the end, public relations head Kevin Shea stood closest to Duquette. Shea had originally been hired during the Gorman years as a bright, personable up-and-comer but as time went on, Shea evolved into a Duquette clone and became a too-enthusiastic purveyor of ill will.

In March of 1998, with Mo Vaughn campaigning for a contract extension, the Sox played a Grapefruit League game in Port Charlotte against the Rangers. Vaughn had a good day at the plate and was allowed to take a van back to Fort Myers—this was standard procedure for veterans—before the game ended. Reporters were not allowed in the clubhouse during the game, so we asked Shea if Vaughn could be brought out to the doorway to answer questions.

Shea disappeared for a minute and returned to say that Vaughn didn't want to talk.

Didn't want to talk? Vaughn had never seen a question he didn't want to answer, and this spring especially, was a man on a mission to build public support for his staying in Boston. This was preposterous, but Shea had a squad of local deputy sheriffs outside of the clubhouse and there was no way to get to Vaughn.

The next day, I asked Vaughn why he didn't want to talk to us.

"Who told you that? He's a liar. I never told anyone I didn't want to talk," Vaughn roared.

When he found out that it was Shea, Vaughn simply shook his head and said, "It figures." I tracked Shea down and told him what Vaughn said. We eventually had a loud argument in an equipment room, since Shea wanted no part of being exposed in the clubhouse setting.

During that ugly month of September 2000, communication seemed to have broken down between Williams and Duquette. Williams fell back on his "We'll keep things in-house" response while Duquette refused to be interviewed. We asked Shea for some sort of team comment, to which he disdainfully replied, "If they have spoken in the last 24 hours, it's nobody's business. It's nobody in this press box's business."

The Duquette regime was toppled shortly after John Henry's ownership group took over in February of 2002. Duquette had tried for eight years to bring a world championship to Boston, stepping on toes and making enemies at every turn.

It took the new bosses, making friends and building bridges along the way, just three years to erase the awful stain that they had inherited.

# SNAPSHOT

## Maurice Samuel Vaughn

Mo Vaughn was very good at making entrances.

He first entered the consciousness of Red Sox fans with a memorable speech in January of 1991. He first entered the consciousness of American League pitchers on June 30 of that year with a home run that almost knocked down Baltimore's Memorial Stadium before Camden Yards was finished.

Vaughn wore a Boston uniform from the middle of the 1991 season through the final game of the 1998 playoffs. In

those years he established himself as one of the most significant figures in franchise history, a strong-willed, articulate,
intelligent, thoughtful African-American player, the type of
player that terrified the Yawkey ownership.

Vaughn was not the first such man to play for the Sox.
Earl Wilson, Reggie Smith and Tommy Harper preceded
him, but all were ahead of their time and none was
embraced the way that Vaughn was. Vaughn became more
than just a good player. He became the public face of the
Red Sox clubhouse.

His public debut happened at the annual Boston BaseBall
Writers dinner in January, 1991. Vaughn had been voted Red
Sox Minor League Player of the Year for his strong season in
Pawtucket and as such was invited to make a few remarks.
His speech came late in the evening. As a head table guest,
Vaughn was entitled to open bar privileges and took advan-
tage of them, and by the time he ascended to the podium was
in a delightful mood.

What followed was an acceptance speech like no one had
ever heard before. Vaughn bounced from topic to topic, cir-
cling the baseball globe along the way. He spoke with such
good-natured sincerity that eventually, an entire banquet hall
of 1,200 people was laughing uproariously, and collectively,
not sure exactly why.

That speech marked Vaughn as someone to keep an eye
on, and he didn't disappoint. He was called up to the majors
from Pawtucket on June 27 and was 2 for 9 as a major leaguer
when he came up to bat in the bottom of the sixth on June 30
in Baltimore.

Orioles starter Jeff Robinson threw Vaughn a fastball that
he hit on a line to right field. The ball was searing more than

soaring as it headed toward the bleachers, slicing through the air in the direction of Memorial Stadium's back wall. It hit some four rows shy of that back wall and was one of the longest home runs ever seen at the old ballpark.

I went out to the bleachers after everyone had calmed down to talk to the fans out there. They reported that it was an absolutely terrifying experience, hearing the ball come towards them like a sizzling cheeseburger with wings. It landed in the middle of a group of off-duty policemen, all of whom scattered rather than try to catch it. By all accounts, it was probably the second longest home run ever hit at Memorial Stadium, surpassed only by the great Frank Robinson.

While Vaughn arrived in the majors in less than three seasons as a pro, it took him a while to get comfortable. But when he did, he quickly became the unofficial team leader, a job he welcomed. This was a major change from the strong, silent type of leadership Sox teams of the past had followed.

In 1994, for example, the Red Sox acquired outfielder Wes Chamberlain from the Phillies. Chamberlain was an excellent athlete who could hit for power, but had never lived up to his potential. He was introverted to the point of being sullen and Vaughn tried hard to steer him in a different direction.

Chamberlain arrived on May 31 and one night not long after that, the Sox lost a game at Fenway in which Vaughn made errors that led to the defeat. Vaughn's locker was in the far corner of the clubhouse, diagonal from the manager's office, a spot reserved for players like Jim Rice in the past.

When Vaughn came out of the shower, he saw a bunch of reporters waiting for him and said to them, "Gentlemen, follow me." He escorted them up to where Chamberlain was getting dressed, sat down on an empty stool next to the new outfielder, and began a monologue that opened with "You can blame me for losing this game."

It was an unambiguous message for Chamberlain, and anyone else within earshot, that this is the way we deal with things here when we screw up.

Vaughn won the league Most Valuable Player Award for his performance in 1995, edging the Indians' Albert Belle. The MVP voting is strictly for regular-season performance, and a good thing. Vaughn was awful in the playoffs, going 0 for 14 with seven strikeouts as Cleveland swept the Sox in the Division Series.

By 1998, he was on his way out of town as free agency loomed. He had gotten heavier through the years, as had Roger Clemens for that matter, and the Sox were afraid that Vaughn's weight could cause him problems down the road. They wouldn't admit that, but Vaughn had a "Who's kidding whom?" press conference about the issue in which he said that they had told him to his face that they were worried about his weight.

He started his final season in Boston in dramatic fashion. The Red Sox hit the road to open the season and were 3-5 on a West Coast trip. They came home to face Randy Johnson and the Seattle Mariners on April 10, 1998 and went into the last of the ninth trailing, 7-2. Mariners manager Lou Piniella took out Johnson after eight. In the ninth, the Sox faced three consecutive relievers with past or future Boston connections—Heathcliff Slocumb, Tony Fossas and Mike Timlin—and cut the lead to 7-5.

Piniella brought in lefty Paul Spoljaric to face Vaughn with the bases loaded—why managers did this was beyond

comprehension since he hit lefties as well as he hit righties—
and Vaughn won the game with a walkoff grand slam.

Boston qualified for the playoffs as the wild card team,
which gave Vaughn a chance to take care of his final piece of
unfinished business with the Sox. He erased the memory of
that 1995 post-season failure by going 7 for 17 (.412) with two
home runs and 7 RBIS in the Division Series versus
Cleveland.

Vaughn signed with the Angels in the off-season. The Red
Sox didn't fall apart without him. They made post-season
play again in 1999 and actually went a round further than
they ever had with him in the lineup. And Vaughn's career
did not end when he left, even though out on the West Coast,
he sort of dropped from sight. He had two big seasons in
Anaheim before going to the Mets where, finally, injuries
forced him from the game.

But not from the memory of anyone who heard that first
speech, or saw that first home run in Baltimore.

# The Kennedy Administration

IN THE LONG AFTERMATH OF THEIR 1918 WORLD SERIES VICTORY, the Red Sox had never won when they were expected to. Each pennant came as a complete surprise—1946 after the uncertain war years; 1967 after eight straight losing seasons; 1975 after the fold of 1974; and 1986 after seven seasons of non-contending.

And so it was again in 1995.

The players strike that caused 1994 to be the Year Without a World Series did not end until the spring of 1995. That left every team scrambling to put something together after a ridiculous spring training that involved something politely called "replacement players."

Nobody scrambled better than the Red Sox, where Dan Duquette perfected the flea market method of constructing a team. In the span of one week after the strike was settled in early April, Duquette signed catcher Mike Macfarlane, DH Reggie Jefferson and pitchers Stan Belinda, Erik Hanson and Zane Smith as free agents. Then, on April 14 Duquette claimed outfielder Troy O'Leary when the Brewers exposed him to waivers.

Gone were the remnants of the 1994 disaster, including Hobson, who was fired and replaced as manager by Kevin Kennedy. Duquette had made off-season trades, as well, in anticipation of the end of the strike, and southpaw pitcher Rheal Cormier, second baseman Luis Alicea and slugger Jose Canseco were among the new faces.

The season did not begin until April 26. When it did, Boston won its first three games and then, after crushing the Tigers on May 7, 12-1, went into first place for good. The Sox eventually built an obscenely large lead that peaked on August 24 at 15 ½ games, and they did it in completely unorthodox fashion. Duquette ran what amounted to an ongoing tryout camp. Kennedy took whatever the GM sent him and kept winning.

The Red Sox were Kennedy's second major league team. He had been an unsuccessful catcher in the minors, but became a very successful minor league manager in the Dodgers organization. Kennedy then moved on to Montreal, where he worked with Duquette in administration, then became Felipe Alou's bench coach.

That eventually led to Kennedy being hired to manage the Texas Rangers, whom he was with in 1993 and 1994. He was best remembered as the manager who let Canseco pitch in a blowout game in 1993, the result being that Canseco blew out his right elbow and missed most of the season.

The 1995 Red Sox were a Hollywood Squares team, and Kennedy was the perfect host for their show.

Canseco was a country unto himself. During his years in Oakland, he had gone from being a *Baseball America* cover story to being on the cover of *People Magazine*. He dated Madonna, owned cars that cost way too much and drove them way too fast, and was likely to walk into the Red Sox clubhouse dressed all in yellow like something that had escaped from the aviary at the Franklin Park Zoo.

Canseco also talked as if he were interviewing himself. Ask him if he thought he could hit 500 home runs before his career was over and he'd respond, "Sure, because I'm big and strong and know what I am doing." And yet, he was a popular man in the clubhouse because his ego was so big that he was bulletproof. Teammates would make fun of the way he dressed and talked and Canseco would laugh along with them. He was what Babe Ruth must have been like, a man with one thousand best friends, none of whose names he knew.

Then there were Vaughn and Clemens, major forces of their own. With Vaughn finally delivered from the uneasy truce that had existed between him and Hobson, the first baseman blossomed into one of the game's most formidable forces. Clemens, whose brilliant career had stagnated during the Hobson years, had a sore right shoulder and started the season on the disabled list. With Canseco and Vaughn dominating the news, Clemens was able to stay more in the shadows and work on re-establishing his career.

Kennedy's ego was a big as any in the Boston clubhouse. Tall and muscular, Kennedy was always impeccably dressed and immaculately groomed. The manager's office at Fenway Park is not much of an improvement over a monk's cell at a monastery, except that the shower and toilet both have doors. Managers came and went so fast with the Sox that nothing permanent was ever hung on the walls. About the only change in décor was whatever brand of shaving cream a new manager chose to put on the shelf over the sink.

However, Kennedy decorated the corner office. His theme was Entertainment Tonight, with pictures of B-level Hollywood movie starlets and Country & Western singers lining the walls. Aside from that, the office was just short of a shrine to the late Natalie Wood, whom it was fair to say was Kennedy's favorite actress.

The new manager was not an egalitarian. He treated stars like Canseco differently than role players, and made no apologies for it. Kennedy loved establishing his importance with reporters by keeping them waiting endlessly. Scheduled 3:30 P.M. interview sessions would wind up starting at 5:00, or he would simply have us wait outside the closed door of his office like loved ones hovering around the door of the emergency room waiting for news of a car accident.

Kennedy was not afraid to be critical. His favorite response was,

"This is not player development" when talking about mistakes. He liked to have people think that he knew about everything that was going on everywhere. You could ask him if he knew that the population of Winnipeg, Manitoba had fallen by 4.2 percent in the last 10 years and Kennedy would reply, "I was aware of it."

He once told a group of rather stunned reporters that he took at least six showers a day, and that clinical studies had proven that people who took a lot of showers were successful people. Kennedy said that doctors had told him he was in the top two percent of fast healers. He once closed the clubhouse before a game to hold a meeting on nutritional supplements, which turned out to be nothing more than a pitch session for a product called Met-Rx, which Kennedy had more than a scientific interest in.

Still, although he was hardly loveable, Kennedy was an excellent manager. He knew exactly how to employ his players to get the most out of them, was unafraid to make unorthodox moves and had an excellent sense of game strategy.

While Vaughn and Canseco were the headliners as the Sox dominated the AL East, players like Hanson, Macfarlane, Belinda, O'Leary and Alicea made unexpected contributions. Hanson was unbeatable in the early weeks and went on to have the best season of his career. Macfarlane was not a gifted catcher, but brought a scrap-iron competitiveness to the position that made him more valuable than his statistics would have indicated. O'Leary started out as a bench player, but every time he got into the lineup, delivered big hits and eventually became a regular.

Alicea was a switch-hitter with a little power and a solid fielder. He was outgoing and funny and fit in nicely in the relaxed atmosphere that Kennedy fostered in the clubhouse. Alicea also provided one of the season's most entertaining non-baseball stories.

He lived in Florida and owned horses, and one time took some acquaintances to visit the horses. A woman asked if she could feed one of them and Alicea said sure, horses love being fed and are very gentle, so just give him a carrot or something—but be careful, since their teeth can be dangerous.

The next thing he knew, Alicea heard his name being called. "Luis . . . Luis . . . your horse just bit off my finger" his guest cried, and Alicea figured it was just a joke until he looked at his friend's hand and, sure enough, the top of one of her fingers was gone. "I told you to be careful," he said.

Talk about being the perfect host.

With Clemens out early, the Sox struggled to find enough pitching. They used people like Brian Looney, Mike Hartley and Keith Shepherd, but lack of pitching depth threatened to ruin the good start. So Duquette hit the yard sales again.

On April 27, just as the season started, he signed knuckle ball pitcher Tim Wakefield to a minor league contract, then brought him up to the majors exactly a month later. Three days after that, Duquette signed veteran reliever Mike Maddux, brother of Greg.

Wakefield had been the best story of the 1992 season while with the Pirates. He was called up from Triple A in the middle of the season and went 8-1 for Pittsburgh, throwing the knuckle ball almost exclusively, and then won two games in the NLCS. And that seemed to be it, Wakefield's 15 minutes of fame. He was back in the minors two seasons later, and not only was he back in the minors, he was awful. In 1994, Wakefield was the worst pitcher in Triple A, going 5-15 for the Pirates' farm team in Buffalo. Pittsburgh finally released him during spring training in 1995, after which Duquette decided to take a chance on him.

Wakefield started the season in Pawtucket and was very, very good. The Red Sox hit the West Coast in late May, their starting rotation in shambles, and Wakefield flew into Anaheim to start the May 27 game against the Angels. He won it, 12-1. Kennedy decided to gamble again and had Wakefield start in Oakland on May 30, working on just two days rest, and he beat the A's, 1-0.

It was the beginning of a series of performances that were reminiscent of what Clemens had done in 1986, or what Carl Yastrzemski had done with the bat in 1967. On June 4, in his third start for Boston, and first at Fenway Park, Wakefield pitched against the Mariners and took a 0-0 game into the 10th, where he gave up an unearned run. In the last of the 10th, O'Leary hit a two-run homer into the screen to salvage the win.

In his first 17 starts, Wakefield went 14-1, finally fading a bit in the closing weeks to finish at 16-8.

The addition of Maddux—who gave up a three-run homer on his first pitch as a Red Sox—was not quite so dramatic, but he turned out to be a key member of the bullpen. He had been released by the Pirates and was at home, and the Sox actually sent scouts out to his house to watch him throw before signing him, and it took a while for them to finally make up their minds.

Kennedy was constantly quizzed on the status of the Maddux negotiations, the questions culminating in an odd exchange between TV analyst Bob Montgomery and the manager. Montgomery tried to nail down if Kennedy had actually seen Maddux throw, or at least talked to him in person. Finally, the exasperated announcer asked, "So, let's see if I've got this straight. You haven't actually met with him—facially?"

And Kennedy had to admit that, no, he and Maddux had yet to meet facially. However, they did so not long after that.

Maddux was a middle reliever and spot starter, and as the season went on the Red Sox' most pressing need became someone to help Belinda finish out games. On July 6, Duquette traded pitcher Frankie Rodriguez, a former top draft pick who had turned out to be a waste of time, to the Twins for Rick Aguilera. Boston might not have needed Aguilera save for the ongoing inconsistency of Ken Ryan, who had never quite caught on as a closer.

In 1995, Ryan was once again up and down. In July, he was down, sent to Double A Trenton, and while there took the team bus to Binghamton, New York for a series with the Mets farm club there.

In a business where many players gave lip service to the idea of being family men, Ryan was passionately devoted to his. While he was in the minors, his family was back home in Massachusetts, and while he was in Binghamton, Ryan got a call from home saying that his wife was going into premature labor.

There were no planes going out of Binghamton that night, no trains and no buses that would get him home fast enough, and walking was out of the question. So, Ryan called a taxi, and headed back to New England on what had to be one of the longest cab rides in history.

The final tab, including tip, was $350.

By the beginning of August, the only question was how much Boston would win the division by, and who the Sox would play in the post-season, which would be the first one under the new playoff plan that included a wild-card team. They clinched the division title on September 20 and found out that their opponent in the division series would be the Indians.

The Sox' last two visits to the post-season had resulted in four-game sweeps by the Athletics, and this visit was only slightly better. The series was best of five and Boston was swept in three games. Vaughn, a controversial winner of the American League MVP over Cleveland's Albert Belle, had a disastrous series, going 0 for 14 with seven strikeouts.

The first game went 13 innings and was memorably disappointing. It was 3-3 after nine, then Tim Naehring homered in the 11th to make it 4-3. Aguilera, who had really been acquired specifically for the post-season, gave the lead right back in the last of the 11th when Belle hit one out. The Indians won it in the 13th when Tony Pena, by now at the end of the line and a last-measure backup catcher, hit a home run off Smith.

The Sox went down meakly in the next two games, making it 13 consecutive post-season losses for them going back to the last two games of the 1986 World Series.

The losing continued, unexpectedly in 1996. As usual, Duquette did a lot of off-season tinkering. The Sox seemed to be a bit short of pitching, and at a cookout in Fort Myers following the annual BC-Red Sox exhibition game, Joe Morgan, former manager and a Boston College graduate, asked the GM about Boston's perceived lack of depth on the mound.

"We think we've got enough power to make up for it," Duquette said, to which Morgan responded, "Yeah, you'd think so, but it doesn't work that way."

Nor did it. When the regular season opened in early April, three key members of the 1995 team—Alicea, Macfarlane and Hanson—were gone. And by mid-April, so were any hopes of an AL East title repeat.

The Red Sox got off to their worst start since the Bob Quinn days. They went 3-16 in their first 19 games. By April 19, Boston was 8 ½ games out of first place and had been outscored, 118-68. The only thing the Sox led the league in was finger-pointing, and it got ridiculous at times.

Kennedy blamed traveling secretary Steve August for scheduling too many exhibition games against the same teams. The Sox' spring training site was in Fort Myers, at the end of the Grapefruit League road, and in order to cut down on long bus trips that made the players unhappy, August scheduled games with the handful of teams that were fairly close. Kennedy also blamed the training staff for not doing a good enough job of keeping Sox players healthy, but that bordered on Nixonian paranoia.

Finally, on April 30, the finger-pointing turned to scapegoat. The Sox fired pitching coach Al Nipper and, of all people, bullpen coach Dave Carlucci, which would be like the president firing the Ambassador to Estonia because the economy had tanked.

Boston's pitching coach situation had, under Kennedy, become "The head bone is connected to the neck bone" stuff. Nipper was replaced by Sammy Ellis, Carlucci by Herm Starrette, a nice guy who had been fired himself as pitching coach during spring training in 1995 and replaced by John Cumberland. Nipper had orginally gotten his job when Cumberland was mysteriously fired midway through 1995. Starrette had been around a bit and seemed a little befuddled by what was going on.

Duquette made some mid-summer moves to salvage something out of the season, the best one being the signing of free-agent second baseman Jeff Frye. On July 31, he traded pitcher Jamie Moyer to Seattle for Darren Bragg, a deal that worked in the short term but was a mistake in the long term.

By Memorial Day, the season had turned into a reminder of what it was like in the 1950s when Ted Williams was the only reason to buy a ticket to watch the Red Sox. This time, the only reason to buy a ticket was Roger Clemens.

It was the final year Clemens was under contract to Boston, and indications were that the Red Sox would not work very hard to keep him. Clemens rose to the challenge, providing two of the season's most memorable moments.

On May 23 at Fenway Park in a game against the Mariners, Kennedy made some lineup moves that took the Designated Hitter out of play. Clemens was pitching, and Kennedy decided to let him get up and hit late in the game. The Rocket Man ripped a single up the middle off of Norm Charlton, and won the game on the mound, 11-4.

Then, in chilly Detroit at decrepit Tiger Stadium on September 18, Clemens made history again by striking out 20 for the second time in his career. The Tigers had no chance that night. Clemens might not have known in which war the Battle of San Juan Hill was fought, but he had a keen sense of baseball history and his place in it. On this night, Clemens took the mound with 191 wins, and 37 shutouts, in a Boston uniform. Those numbers were good for second place in both categories behind Cy Young, who had 192 wins and 38 shutouts. Clemens also had pitched 99 complete games, well behind Young, but just one away from 100.

The final score was 4-0. The final out was a strikeout of Travis Fryman, and Strike Three was Clemens' 151st pitch of the night. Clemens was teary-eyed in his post-game press conference, admitting that while he knew he had a win, and a shutout, he did not know he had fanned 20 again until after the final pitch, when catcher Bill Haselman told him. The Rocket Man stayed at Tiger Stadium until 1 A.M., reflecting on what he had done, before going back to the team hotel in suburban Dearborn.

The next day, true to form, Clemens got up and decided he would run from the Ritz-Carlton out in Dearborn, and down Michigan Avenue to Tiger Stadium, a distance of about 12 miles. Except that those 12 miles were not precisely the economic and social heart of the Detroit area, and trying to make that run would have been like trying to run 12 miles along Omaha Beach on D-Day. The hotel bellman persuaded Clemens not to try it.

In his day-after press conference, the Rocket Man talked about his uncertain future with the Red Sox, and essentially talked about his Boston career in the past tense. One thing was sure, he said—he only wanted to pitch for four more years at most, then retire to spend time with his family.

He was winning Cy Young Awards eight years after that night in Detroit, but not with the Sox. Clemens' Boston career was, indeed, in the past tense after the 20-strikeout game—he did not win another game for the Sox—and what a ride it had been.

He had provided Red Sox fans with the greatest pitching they had ever seen, it being safe to say that no one alive from 1986 to 1996 had seen Young pitch. In an era when starting pitchers began to use the term "I did my job" to describe their six or seven-inning stints every fifth day, Clemens was a pack mule, pitching inning after inning, often in games that meant nothing except to those who had bought tickets.

He was the ultimate definition of a Hall of Fame player, one so good that people paid money solely to see him perform, and Clemens almost always put on a show.

The Rocket Man became almost legendary for his malapropisms. He once said, when asked what usually happened when he had to work on extra rest, "It makes me very erotic." He would confuse words, saying things like, "I've been struggling in all assets of my game." In 1989, at the Hall of Fame game the year that Carl Yastrzemski was inducted, Clemens was asked about Yaz being honored and said, "This is one more nail in his coffin."

Yet, this was the same superstar whom I saw one day in 1995, sitting in a chair in the Fenway Park clubhouse, a huge bucket of mail next to him. Offhandedly, I said, "It'll take you the rest of the year to answer all that mail." To which he replied, quite seriously, "Longer than that. This is from 1992. I answer all of it myself."

With occasional help from Clemens, Kennedy pulled things together enough so that the Red Sox eventually reached .500 in late August. On August 31, rookie Nomar Garciaparra made his big-league debut, coming into a game in Oakland as a second baseman. Another rookie, Trot Nixon, made his first appearance on September 21.

Kennedy was not around to see either of them become regulars. While his contract extended through 1997, the Sox had a September 20 deadline to renew it for 1998 and failed to make an offer. With that, Kennedy knew he would be gone, and he was fired right after the season ended.

Duquette and Kennedy, who had gotten along famously in Montreal, could not get along in Boston. This was no surprise. Neither was very likeable, and Kennedy was a strong-willed manager working for a general manager who liked yes-men.

So Duquette went out and tried to find one, but didn't really succeed.

# Interlude:
# The Red Seat

IT IS FENWAY PARK'S VERSION OF PLYMOUTH ROCK, SMALL AND plain, unexceptional in appearance, but historic beyond description.

Like a comet, it is visible only at certain times, and almost never when there is a baseball game being played. Section 42, Row 37, Seat 21—the Red Seat, where 56-year-old Joseph Boucher was sitting on June 9, 1946, the day he was struck on top of the head by a ball hit by Ted Williams.

It is considered to be the longest home run ever hit at Fenway Park, and one of the longest in baseball history. It is also considered, by most players of the present generation of Red Sox players, to be a fairy tale.

"It is a myth. A myth," former Boston first baseman Mo Vaughn would say with disgust as he watched his longest batting practice home runs fall 25 rows short. "No man can hit a baseball that far."

Day after day, night after night, Red Sox players and opposition players take hundreds of swings in batting practice, then hundreds more in games, and nobody ever comes close to hitting the Red Seat. The hitters gather around the batting cage and gaze out at the Red Seat like they were looking at one of the moons of Neptune and, for the life of them, can't figure out how anyone would be crazy enough to think a baseball can be hit that far.

"I went out and stood at that seat, oh, if not last year, then maybe the year before," said Sox right fielder Trot Nixon, "and nothing against Ted Williams, but I don't see how anyone could hit a ball that far. I've never seen a ball come close, not even in batting practice, and there have been some great hitters here over the years."

Sox broadcaster Jerry Remy was not known for his power when he played second base for Boston, but has played in, or seen, thousands of games at Fenway Park. He, too, is skeptical.

"I've never seen anybody come close to it," says Remy. "The longest ball I've ever seen hit here was by Eddie Murray, and he hit it to the runway in center field, the one back behind the bullpen, and that's not nearly as high as where the Red Seat is. I remember, as a player, seeing home runs hit out there and saying to myself 'Whoa'— and as a player, you don't have that reaction very often—and those home runs land maybe five rows over the bullpens."

Anyone who ever stands out at the Red Seat and looks back towards home plate has to be struck by how far away it seems. Armed with that first-hand impression, and with the input from players, all of whom seem to think the seat is a myth, this reporter set out to debunk the Red Seat story and set the record straight.

The quest started with owner John Henry.

"I've been out there," Henry said, "and it is hard to believe, I know." Henry was asked if he would have any objections to having the distance measured. Unlike the previous paranoids who ran the team, and who would have been reluctant to divulge the location of Fenway's ketchup dispensers, Henry thought it was a great idea.

"Do whatever you have to do," he said, "and we'll help any way we can."

The Red Sox media guide lists the Red Seat as being 502 feet from home plate. Former Sox manager Joe Morgan, during his tenure in the Rectangular Office, once measured it at 519 feet. It looks closer to 519 than 502, and it is. The measurement done for this story, while not done as precisely as a surveyor might do it, was done carefully and has the seat at about 514 feet from the plate.

The spot where the ball hit Mr. Boucher's head was measured at about 33 feet above field level.

So, picture this: For a right-handed batter to hit a ball as far as the Red Seat, the Green Monster would have to be moved back 200 feet, with the ball hitting four feet from the top of it.

While common sense and the opinions of major-league baseball players say that the Red Seat must be mythical, its existence, and placement, is grounded in the reality of eyewitness observations. While there is no film or videotape of the home run, and not even any still pictures, there are newspaper accounts of the event, and there is Johnny Pesky.

Pesky was the Red Sox shortstop that day and recalls the home run very clearly.

"Actually," he said, "what I remember most is the sound. The crack of the bat sounded like a cannon shot. And the ball took off the way a rocket does, and just carried and carried."

The Tigers pitcher for that game was Fred Hutchinson, who was much more John Burkett than Roger Clemens, meaning that Williams had to provide most of his own power.

"Hutchinson was a breaking-ball pitcher," Pesky said. "He threw just hard enough to set up his breaking ball."

In a 1996 interview with Dan Shaughnessy of the *Boston Globe*, Williams said he hit a changeup. Given Williams' legendary recall of the details of his home runs, it seems safe to say that Hutchinson threw him a changeup.

There were six daily newspapers in Boston in 1946 and all of them covered the game. One, the *Traveler*, only mentioned the home run in passing. The other five were more detailed in their descriptions, but there are some differences in their accounts.

The *Herald* said the ball landed about halfway up the bleachers and estimated the distance at 500 feet. The *Record* called it the longest home run ever seen at Fenway and estimated it landed between 25 and 30 rows up, as did the *American*. The *Post* reported that the ball landed two-thirds of the way up, but said the bleachers contained 60 rows, when there actually are slightly fewer than 50.

The most detailed account of the Red Seat shot was in the *Globe*. Reporter Harold Kaese interviewed Boucher, who said, "The sun was right in our eyes. All we could do is duck. I'm glad I didn't stand up. They say it bounced a dozen rows higher, but after it hit my head, I was no longer interested."

Kaese identified Boucher's seat as being in Section 42, Row 33, directly next to the aisle and said it was a bit more than halfway up the bleachers. That is different from where the Red Sox have located the Red Seat and a cause for some confusion, and that issue will be dealt with in a bit. Oddly, even though Kaese had the most exact placement of where the ball landed, he estimated it as traveling only 450 feet.

While there were are no photographs of the home run itself, there is one of Mr. Boucher and his hat, and it shows a hole directly in the middle of the top of the straw hat, indicating that the ball was descending almost straight down.

There were also two cartoonists at the game. The *Globe* cartoon has the ball landing just above the runway behind the bullpen. The *Post* cartoon has it landing at almost the exact spot the Red Seat is at today, perhaps a smidgen lower.

So, by all accounts, Williams' home run was an exceptional one, and unquestionably the longest one ever hit to that part of the ballpark. But did it really go that far or is it, as Vaughn contended, a myth?

The most logical answer seems to be that the Red Seat is not a myth, but is probably a slight exaggeration, and much of the answer lies in the weather on that early June afternoon.

On the day before, New England had been wracked by a weather system that produced vicious hailstorms. As it moved out to sea, a contrasting system of very dry air moved in. As often happens, the change in air produced a fierce prevailing wind. That afternoon, the weather at Fenway included a 20 mph tailwind unusually strong with temperatures in the mid-70s and very low humidity. In other words, it was a perfect day to hit.

So perfect, in fact, that Red Sox center fielder Dom DiMaggio, a right-handed batter who was just 5 feet 9 inches and weighed 168 pounds, and who hit just four home runs at Fenway Park in that entire 1946 season, homered into what is now the Boston bullpen.

To take a more scientific look at the Red Seat homer, we had two assistant professors of physics at Holy Cross, Matthew Koss and Timothy Roach, look at the numbers. Both baseball fans, they created a spreadsheet and ran different scenarios through it. They came up with this:

"The best bet is that Ted Williams pulled a changeup into a 20 mph tailwind at a launch angle of 30 to 35 degrees and at 117-118 mph. Therefore, if the ball were allowed to continue from where it landed in the seats, it would have gone an additional 28 to 34 feet for a total of 542 to 548 feet from home plate."

There has been some work done on the physics of baseball which indicates that 550 feet is probably the far edge of how far a ball can be hit, and 120 mph is probably the far edge of how fast a batted ball can travel. Given all that, Williams' colossal home run is at the far edge of possibility but a possibility, nonetheless.

"I have to say that it can't be ruled out," Koss said. Koss is troubled by the fact that Williams hit a changeup, meaning that the speed of the pitched ball was of little help. What probably made the remarkable distance of the Red Seat home run possible was the wind. It had a huge effect. In fact, on a day with no wind, DiMaggio's home run, for instance, would have traveled 50 feet less and been just an easy out in right-center.

So, it would appear that the Red Seat homer was the Fenway equivalent of the Blizzard of 1978, the Perfect Storm, the USA's hockey gold medal in 1980, or even Bob Beamon's record-shattering long jump in the 1968 Olympics—a once-a-century confluence of all sorts of favorable factors that produced unimaginable results.

There remains one nagging question. How did the Red Seat come to be in Row 37, Seat 21? And nobody seems to know. The Fenway bleachers were remodeled 20 years ago, the wooden benches that Mr. Boucher sat on being replaced by individual seats. But the 30-inch wide concrete steps that the seats were bolted to have not changed. There are the same number of rows in 2003 as there were in 1946.

If measurements are made from the seat closest to the aisle on Row 33, not 37, guess what? The distance comes to 502½ feet from home plate, almost exactly what the Red Sox say is how far Williams' home run traveled. Putting the Red Seat there, according to Koss and Roach's figures, would have the home run going a maximum distance of 526 to 532 feet, a much more believable figure.

So, could the current placement of the the Red Seat be a simple mistake in translating Kaese's story?

At this point, that seems to be the most likely scenario. While the Red Sox should definitely move the Red Seat to the end of whatever row it is in, they should also consider finding out why it is currently in Row 37 as opposed to Row 33.

Nixon suggests that there is a way to put an end to the mystery, and that's by having the Sox bring in someone like Barry Bonds to try and duplicate the smash. Charge fans, say, $25 a head to watch, and give the money to charity.

That sounds good, but under current conditions, Williams' blast may be impossible to duplicate. Prior to the 1990 season, what is now called the .406 Club was built, blocking at least part of any sort of tailwind that might arise on a given day. That change in the tailwind factor could account for why none of today's Red Sox hitters can come close to the Red Seat no matter what the weather.

The definitive book on home runs is *The Home Run Encyclopedia*, edited by Bob McConnell and David Vincent, and published by the

Society of American Baseball Research in 1996. In that book, researcher William J. Jenkinson concludes that most of the legendary long home runs of the past are exaggerations. A prime example is Mickey Mantle's famous home run in Washington, D.C. in 1953. It was reported to have traveled 565 feet, but that was the distance where the ball was retrieved, not where it landed. It hit the earth at about 510 feet, then bounced and rolled.

At the Row 37 placement, Williams' home run may indeed be the longest in the history of baseball. Even at Row 33, which seems to be a minimum distance, it remains one of the most epic blasts in the history of the game. And while today's players may shake their heads in disbelief as they gaze at the tiny red dot in the right-field bleachers, they should remember one thing.

Ted Williams is the man who, on the last day of the 1941 season, went into a doubleheader hitting .3996 and rather than protecting his average, played two games and went 6 for 8 to finish at .406. He is the same man who, also in 1946 at Fenway, became the only player ever to hit a home run off of Rip Sewell's eephus pitch, a softball toss that may have been thrown at something like 50 mph maximum.

The same man who, at age 39 in 1957, batted .388 and the same man who, on a cold, damp, dreary late September day in 1960—the kind of day when nobody can hit a home run to right field at Fenway Park—took the last swing of his life and put a ball into the Red Sox bullpen.

The Red Seat?

It is not a myth, Mo Vaughn, even if it does appear to be a slight exaggeration. It is just a little bit larger than life, as was the hitter who created it.

# Jimy Williams and the Light at the End of the Tunnel

BEFORE REPLACING KEVIN KENNEDY AS MANAGER, DUQUETTE replaced Sammy Ellis as pitching coach with Joe Kerrigan, another old friend from the Expos days. It was a strange move, since the pitching coach is probably the only important coach on a staff, and a manager often lives or dies with him. With his fate so closely bound to the pitching coach, the manager wants to have some hand in naming one.

Whoever the new manager was knew coming in where he stood on the list of priorities, and had to be comfortable with that, and apparently Jimy Williams was.

Williams had been a manager once previously, in Toronto, and had not done very well there. His 1987 Blue Jays suffered through one of the greatest collapses in history, losing their last seven games of the season to finish two games behind the Tigers. In 1989, Toronto was 12-24 when Williams was fired, then went on to win the AL East title under replacement Cito Gaston.

Since then, Williams had served as Bobby Cox' third base coach in Atlanta and Duquette hoped that whatever it was that made the Braves the best organization in baseball could be transplanted to Boston.

He was wrong—not that it was Williams' fault.

The new manager started the season with a lineup that included Wilfredo Cordero in left field, Shane Mack in center and Rudy Pemberton in right. It was awful. Cordero ran into off-field trouble when he was accused of beating his wife with a telephone; Mack became best known for being one of the few Red Sox players ever to make all of the outs in one inning without hitting into a triple play; and while Pemberton had hit .531 in September of 1996, that turned out to be a freak of statistical nature.

The Sox stumbled in April and never recovered. They finished six games under .500 and just two games out of last place. The dreary summer was best epitomized by what happened in Toronto on June 23. Boston beat the Blue Jays, 7-6, in the first game of what became a three-game sweep. In the second inning, Toronto's Ed Sprague hit a grounder behind the third base bag that Tim Naehring fielded cleanly, then threw to first too late to get Sprague. It was a nice play, typical of Naehring but not far from routine, and it essentially ended his career.

Naehring, a gifted player whose career had already been cruelly short-circuited by a series of unrelated injuries, tore the joint capsule of his right elbow on the throw. Not just tore, actually. It was more like destroyed, and while Naehring stayed in that game, he never played again afterwards.

The injury was initially thought to be relatively minor, but proved to be otherwise. How the Red Sox dealt with it was symptomatic of the curtain of obfuscation that had begun to descend over the franchise. Nobody outside of an operating room had ever heard of a joint capsule, so the Sox were asked to explain what it was. Public relations director Kevin Shea's response was, "A joint capsule is a joint capsule." Trainer Jim Rowe was asked to point to where the joint capsule was and refused to answer.

It didn't matter to Naehring whether or not anyone knew where the joint capsule was. His was destroyed, and so was his career.

The 1997 team was a throwback to the Ted Williams-Bobby Doerr-Vern Stephens teams after World War II. It could hit, but couldn't pitch or catch very well. The Sox almost hit .300 as a team, finishing at .291. In a game in late August in Seattle, they were actually over .300 as a team in the early innings.

A journeyman left-handed hitter, Reggie Jefferson, personified the season. Jefferson was batting .358 in mid-August. It was the highest average in the league, but because he was platooned and did not play against southpaw pitching, he didn't have enough plate appearances to qualify for the batting title.

Jefferson wanted more playing time to make a run at the batting championship and manager Williams obliged. In baseball, less is often more in terms of statistics, and Jefferson should have kept quiet. In the lineup every day, he hit .225 through the end of the season to finish at .319.

Three positive things that came out of 1997 were the emergence of Garciaparra as a star at shortstop; the transformation of Tom Gordon from a mediocre starting pitcher into a very good relief pitcher; and a July 31 trade that wound up being one of the best in Red Sox history. One interesting event, not particularly noteworthy at the time, was the hiring of a long-time, very successful, minor league manager—Grady Little—as Williams' bench coach.

Garciaparra, batting leadoff, had one of the greatest rookie seasons of any Boston player of any era. It was as good overall as Ted Williams in 1939. While Williams hit better, Garciaparra was much better defensively at a much more important position. The rookie shortstop hit .306 with 44 doubles, 11 triples, 30 home runs and 22 stolen bases. He was the first Red Sox player to hit double figures in those four categories since Jackie Jensen had in 1956. Garciaparra's 30-game hitting streak from July 26 to August 29 was the second-longest in franchise history.

Garciaparra quickly became a huge hit with fans. They were not used to seeing this type of player, and the rookie was outgoing, graciously interacting with them and saying that they were the greatest fans in the world at every opportunity. He had a classic baseball name, memorable of itself, and had the little eccentricities and rituals that seemed to be part of the personalities of great players.

Move over, Number 9.

There was a little bit more to Garciaparra than met the eye, though. He was actually an introvert, not at all comfortable in the public domain, and worked hard at creating the image of an affable All-Star because it made life infinitely easier. It was a smart move on his part, and worked for five golden seasons at Fenway.

Gordon was moved to the bullpen in late August and thrived, but this should have been no surprise. Baseball had become closer-centric since the development of the save rule 30 years before, and the history of closers showed that the overwhelming majority were fair-to-lousy starters who found it pretty easy to get three outs when they had been used to getting 21 of them.

In late July, Boston was clearly out of contention, putting the Sox in the strange position of looking to unload veteran players, rather than acquire them for a playoff push. In the Seattle Mariners, Duquette found the perfect sucker. They were willing to take incumbent closer Heathcliff Slocumb and give the Sox two minor leaguers in return, pitcher Derek Lowe and catcher Jason Varitek. Slocumb was an awful relief pitcher, who turned virtually every ninth inning into a James Bond movie, and he did nothing to help Seattle.

Without Lowe and Varitek, it is safe to say, the Red Sox would not have ended their World Series drought at 86 years.

Boston's playoff drought was two years heading into the 1998 season, and Williams had a lot more to work with this time around. In November of 1997, Duquette had traded with the Expos, once again, and this time he got the best starting pitcher in baseball: Pedro Martinez. It was not a deal every team could make—Martinez was getting too expensive for Montreal to keep, and Boston was one of the few teams who could afford him—but Duquette was the one who made it, sending prospects Carl Pavano and Tony Armas Jr. off to Montreal.

The rejuvenated Sox responded by going 92-70, the same record they had in the Impossible Dream season of 1967. But this time, there was no American League pennant as the Yankees won 114 games. No pennant, perhaps, but Boston's record was good enough to qualify for post-season play as the Wild Card team.

Martinez was a large part of the improvement. He did not have as good of a season as he had put together in winning the Cy Young Award in Montreal in 1997, but it was better than what the Sox had been getting out of Clemens in his last few seasons in town. Martinez had 18 wins heading into September and could only get to 19. His ERA was 2.89—good, but not sensational—and he gave up 26 home runs.

Still, the Sox rode his back into a playoff series against Cleveland, where they snapped their long post-season losing streak with an 11-3 victory in Game One, then lost the next three for another early exit.

The series was the finale for Vaughn, who had been in the last year of his contract. He had wanted to sign early, then as the season rolled along, began telling anyone who would listen, "The price goes up every day." The price really didn't matter, as it turned out. Duquette used essentially the same negotiating strategy with Vaughn as he had with Clemens in 1996—make an offer just low enough so the player would not sign, but high enough to make him look greedy when he turned it down.

Duquette replaced Vaughn with Jose Offerman for the 1999 season. Offerman might not drive in as many runs, or hit as many homers as Vaughn, but his offensive presence would be similar—or so the GM said. And he was right for about two weeks. Offerman went 14 for 29 in his first six games in a Boston uniform, was an All-Star in 1999, then became the ultimate specialist, a big-money, low-production infielder who was excellent at catching pop-ups.

Garciaparra continued to get better and better and by 1999 had made the transformation from promising young player to stardom. Martinez followed up his very good 1998 season with a Cy Young season, going 23-4. Nixon—blunt, at times ornery, a bit stubborn and as tough as flank steak—finally got to the majors for good and hit .270, but only after Williams stuck with him through a 2 for 31 start.

At a point where it seemed as though Sox ownership could do nothing right, along came a chance to change that perception, and Harrington and his people took advantage of it on July 13. The All-Star Game was scheduled for Fenway Park for the first time since 1961, and the Red Sox outdid themselves. The circumstances were perfect, since Martinez was the starting pitcher for the American League—opposed by Curt Schilling of the Phillies, no less—and Martinez struck out the first four National League batters he faced.

The AL won, 4-1, but Martinez' performance wasn't even the highlight of the evening. That came pre-game when what was called the All-Century Team—the greatest gathering of baseball talent in the last one hundred years—was assembled on the field. As each baseball legend was introduced, the drama and emotion built. Finally, Ted Williams was driven out onto the diamond in a utility cart and threw out the ceremonial first pitch.

He lingered on the mound, an All-Star of All-Stars, as players from the past and present did homage. Finally, Williams was driven away for what turned out to be one final time.

Boston was in first place in early June, then went into a slump against the National League teams. They never were quite able to catch the Yankees.

In a game against Baltimore on September 25, as the season was winding down, Garciaparra was hit on the right wrist by a pitch from Alberto Reyes. This was not unexpected—Garciaparra crowded the plate, which was one of the reasons why he was such a good hitter—and he was always at risk to get hit when a pitcher came inside.

The wrist hurt, and Garciaparra got some time off in the season's final few days to let it rest for the playoffs. That seemed to do the trick, for he went 13 for 32 (.406) in the post-season.

Again, Boston was the Wild Card team and again played the Indians in the first round of the post-season. By now, this was getting monotonous, particularly since Cleveland tended to make quick and easy work of the Sox. And it seemed like more of the same in 1999 as the Indians beat Boston in the first two games at Jacobs Field. Worse yet, the Red Sox had a 2-0 lead in Game One when Martinez had to leave early with a painful pulled muscle behind his right shoulder. They wound up losing, 3-2, and with the possibility that Martinez was done for the year looming over them, lost again the next night, 11-1.

The series came to Boston with the Sox having been outscored in the first two games, 14-3, and having hit .183 as a team. But they got a lift in Game 3 from Pedro's older brother Ramon Martinez and their bats came to life in a 9-3 win. The next night they won in historic fashion, pounding out 24 hits in a 23-7 victory at Fenway.

Game 5 was in Cleveland the next night, October 11, and it was one of the most compelling games any team in the Boston franchise's long history ever played.

Bret Saberhagen, a Duquette yard sale pickup who had given Boston a fairly good regular season, took his tired, old, aching shoulder out to the Jacobs Field mound and was hammered for five runs in less than two innings, then Lowe came on in relief and gave up three more. But the Sox refused to fold and pounded Indians starter Charles Nagy, the winning pitcher in that long-ago no-hitter thrown by Matt Young in old Cleveland Stadium. O'Leary hit a grand slam in the third to give Boston the lead, then the Indians came back. It was 8-8 going into the last of the fourth, and as Cleveland prepared to hit, Martinez walked in slowly from the bullpen to take the mound.

With his right shoulder still sore from the pulled muscle,

Martinez threw six no-hit innings at the Tribe. O'Leary hit another home run, a three-run job this time, in the seventh and the Red Sox took a 12-8 lead into the last of the ninth. Martinez set the Indians down in order, striking out Omar Vizquel to end the series. Martinez looked to the heavens in thanks, then was mobbed by his teammates.

A year later, Martinez said that as he warmed up to come into the game, he was bombarded with racial epithets and a death threat from Indians fans seated near the Sox bullpen in right field. Among other things, he was called a "beaner," and that was one of the printable descriptions. Despite that, and despite his pain, he turned in Boston's best post-season pitching performance since Jim Lonborg's one-hitter in the 1967 World Series.

The comeback victory sent the Sox into the ALCS for the first time since 1990 and set up the first ever post-season meeting between Boston and the Yankees, what with the 1978 playoff being considered Game 163 of the regular season. New York won far too easily, 4 games to 1, the one Red Sox victory being a 13-1 slaughter at Fenway in a game where the starting pitchers were Pedro Martinez and Roger Clemens, Clemens in his first season as a member of the Yankees.

The Yankees clinched the pennant on October 18 at Fenway, beating the Sox, 6-1. It was to be the last post-season game involving Boston for almost four years. By the time the Red Sox were in the playoffs again, two managers had come and gone, and a third was on his way out.

If Duquette had an ounce of empathy in his heart, he would have fired Williams in the winter of 1999-2000 rather than subject him to the next one-plus seasons of managing the Red Sox. The 2000 and 2001 seasons were tumultuous, stressful, embarrassing years for the Boston organization.

Ownership was preparing to sell the franchise and the farm system had dried up. To plug the inevitable holes on the field, the Sox signed sociopaths and has-beens. Because Martinez was so good, Boston was able to stay in contention. Another key factor was that Williams excelled at getting the best out of a mediocre bunch.

The first sign that Duquette had lost touch was a December 1999 trade of two players with the same last name. He sent prospect Adam Everett to Houston for outfielder Carl Everett, a gifted player with a malignant personality who was not yet 30 years old, but was already on his fifth major-league organization. Everett could be one of the most delightful people in sneakers, and was for much of the time. Cross him, though, and he became a Rottweiler, the ultimate in mutually exclusive terms a vindictive, vicious born-again Christian.

For half a season, things went smoothly. Everett was the team's best position player through the All-Star break and then, as the weather warmed in July, so did Everett's temper. On July 2 in Chicago, he berated *Boston Globe* reporter Dan Shaughnessy with one of the most vile, profanity-laden tirades ever heard in a Boston clubhouse. Everett, who pointed to the heavens during his home run trots, didn't point towards the Almighty at any time during his sickening outburst. Then, in mid-July, one of Everett's old teams came to Fenway Park, the Mets. During a game on July 15, home plate umpire Ron Kulpa warned Everett that he was standing too close to home plate when the center fielder first came to bat in the second inning. With the white chalk line defining the batter's box having long since been obliterated, Kulpa drew a line in the dirt.

Everett erupted with a ferocious, snarling tirade during which he butted into Kulpa. Everett was ejected from the game and later fined and suspended for 10 games. Through that game, Everett had hit .322 with 24 homers and 69 RBIs. From that point on, he hit just .267 with 10 home runs and 39 RBIs. July 15, 2000 effectively marked the end of Everett as a productive member of the Red Sox.

Everett was not Williams' only problem. Duquette kept sending him lemons that no amount of sugar could turn into lemonade.

During the last week of spring training, the Sox signed ancient third baseman Gary Gaetti, who had once been a feared power hitter. They took Gaetti with them to open the season on the West Coast. He went 0 for 10, then was gone for good.

On July 4, Duquette brought in outfielder Bernard Gilkey, late of the Arizona Diamondbacks. When he arrived in Boston, Gilkey was fresh off of a 1 for 47 slump in Arizona, a slump that had been 0 for 29 before he singled in his final at bat. By now, the Red Sox front office had become so disconnected from any definition of truth that it issued a press release regarding Gilkey's signing, saying the new outfielder was "1 for his last 1." Gilkey fell one hit short of the cycle, a triple, in his Boston debut on the 4th of July in Minnesota, then quickly went back to "1 for his last 1" form.

Gilkey and Troy O'Leary both arrived on the same day, although in O'Leary's case it was a re-arrival. O'Leary had been one of Duquette's best moves, a 1995 waiver claim who had turned into a dangerous left-handed hitter and a decent fielder. When he first arrived in town, O'Leary established himself as a very quiet, but not unfriendly, presence in the clubhouse. As the years passed, though, his personality hardened. He became moody and embittered. Ask him a question and the answer was likely to be "Get the [deuce] away from me," so with time, O'Leary was asked fewer and fewer questions, which seemed to be the way he wanted it.

In 2000, he retreated further and further into his shell. Even on the field he seemed distracted, and by the middle of June was batting only .211, at which time Boston put him on the disabled list for an unspecified problem. The problem was not physical, but the Sox would not be any more specific. Pressed to reveal exactly what was going on with O'Leary, team spokesman Shea would only repeat, mindlessly, "We have followed all of the guidelines set down in the Basic Agreement."

The time off helped O'Leary. He was 6 for 10 in his first two games back and managed to pull his average up to .261 by season's

end, although he never revealed exactly what was going on with the
stint on the DL.

During the winter, Duquette signed minor league slugger Israel
Alcantara as a free agent and he began the season in Pawtucket
before coming to Boston in late June. Alcantara had a couple of starts
under his belt when Williams put him in right field for a game in
Chicago on July 1.

What followed was one of the most inexplicably odd performances
by anyone, anywhere, any time, in a Red Sox uniform. Alcantara
played right field like he was practicing for a Pin-the-Tail-on-the-
Donkey tournament, or at least like the game was being played with
invisible baseballs. Alcantara got a hit, then got thrown out when he
wandered off second base like he was trying to find a contact lens in
the dirt.

After the game, Williams was seething, but refused to say anything about what had happened with Alcantara. Still, for those who
had known him long enough and could read between the lines, it
was obvious that the manager was horrified to have been connected
with such a dreadful display. For Alcantara's part, he begged off
commenting on the grounds that his English was not good enough
even though he had been interviewed, and comfortably, several times
since joining the team.

Duquette refused to demote Alcantara and Williams refused to
play him. Finally, after two weeks had gone by, the manager could
no longer try to exist with a 24-man roster and began to use
Alcantara sporadically, if not enthusiastically.

Three weeks after the Alcantara fiasco, Sean Berry came to town.
Berry had been a decent third baseman in the National League
throughout most of the 1990s but had slipped badly in recent years.
A nice man, Berry signed with the Sox on July 23 and immediately
volunteered to meet with groups and show up at clinics. Williams
put him in the lineup for a game at Fenway versus the Twins on July
24. Boston lost, 4-2, and Berry went 0 for 4 with 2 strikeouts.

Cancel those clinics—Duquette took Berry off of the roster the very next day and his major league career was over. Even Williams had to laugh when asked about Berry, saying, "You'd better not be a new player and 0 for 3 around here," which, for Williams, was about as outspoken as it ever got.

"Nothing fazes us," said pitcher Rheal Cormier, a native of New Brunswick, who always brought a Canadian sensibility to the Wild West Show that the Red Sox had become. "You come in to get [medical] treatment, you come up and go 0 for 3, you come up and you don't pitch a shutout, and you're gone."

Williams also had to deal with issues that were nobody's fault. In the ninth inning on September 8 at Fenway Park, reliever Bryce Florie was hit in the face by a line drive off of the bat of the Yankees' Ryan Thompson. It was the most horrible injury at Fenway since Tony Conigliaro took Jack Hamilton's fastball in the face on August 18, 1967. The sound alone was nauseating, sort of what it would be like hearing a truck drive over a hubbard squash. Visually, it looked as if someone had set off a hand grenade next to Florie's right eye.

The pitcher survived the accident—and at first, there was some question about that, which is how bad it was—but did not pitch again in the majors for nearly a year, and really never got back to the big leagues for good.

With Martinez having a milestone season, Boston went into the season's final weeks. The Red Sox arrived in Detroit in mid-September still mathematically in the Wild Card race, but needing to win almost every game to stay in the race. They won the first two, then took the field for the second game of a doubleheader on September 16 with Steve Ontiveros on the mound.

If that second game had been a horse race, the Sox would have been investigated by the racing commission. Ontiveros had not pitched in a major league game since September 29, 1995 and here he was starting a critical game in the middle of a race to make the play-offs. In that second game, Ontiveros faced ten Tigers batters and gave up six runs on five hits and two walks. He threw two wild pitches and, in that span of ten batters, Detroit hit for the cycle getting singles, doubles, a triple and a home run.

Boston lost, 12-2 then lost the next day, 5-4, and post-season play was not going to be part of autumn 2000, in New England. If it was not a success in the standings, that Detroit doubleheader provided one of the season's few amusing moments when, in Game One, the Comerica Park scoreboard froze, and plate umpire Jim Joyce lost track of the count, then allowed Garciaparra to get a single on a 4-2 pitch.

Between games, Joyce came out of the umpires' dressing room and took his medicine like a man, with grace and good humor. "I was looking for divine instruction, but nobody reached out to help me. I'm sure Nomar was happy to get an extra pitch to hit, and I end up with egg on my face."

Boston returned home near the end of September, but the Year 2000 continued its merciless assault on the pysche of Williams, and beyond that, for Red Sox fans in general. Once again, Everett was at the center of things. He said he had a strained left quadricep, but not everyone believed him. He argued with teammate Darren Lewis, then had a closed-door meeting in Williams' office in which he went after the manager the same way he had gone after Shaughnessy. It was loud enough so everyone could hear it, and it was revolting to listen to.

In its aftermath, Duquette refused to criticize Everett. Instead, he essentially said that Everett's obvious abilities excused him from having to follow the rules of civilized behavior.

This was too much for even the reticent Williams to take.

The manager had been the perfect soldier since being hired in 1997. During the round of interviews for the job in the wake of Kevin Kennedy's firing, one of Duquette's Frequently Asked Questions was how a prospective candidate would handle the news media. The preferred answer was "Not tell them anything" and Williams had perfected that technique.

Williams had developed an ability to respond to questions he did not want to answer with something that *Boston Globe* reporter Gordon Edes termed "Jimywocky." Williams would start his response with some general reference to what had been asked, then take the answer down the cellar stairs, up through the bulkhead, into the backyard and out through the woods into the wilderness.

When he was finished, not only did nobody know what the answer was—nobody remembered what the question had been. Since he rarely said anything funny, interesting, or insightful, it was easy to get the impression that Williams didn't really know what was going on. It was just the opposite. He was a tremendous manager, the most knowledgeable person in the Boston dugout since Morgan. He just didn't want anyone to know that.

A good example of how Williams worked happened in Montreal on July 15. In the sixth inning of a tight game against the Expos, Hideo Nomo was on the mound for the Sox with men on base and Orlando Cabrera at bat. Nomo worked the count to 1 and 2, then Williams came out and made a pitching change, calling for Rich Garces.

The move worked in that Garces got Cabrera out and Boston went on to win the game. Afterwards, in the manager's post-game news conference, I asked Williams about the move and he brushed off the question with his most frequent response, "Manager's decision."

Every decision in baseball, just about, is a manager's decision and that response was irksome. I walked out of Williams' office and didn't bother with the rest of the news conference. The next day, when Williams saw me at the ballpark, he asked me to walk out onto the field with him and explained why he made the move.

Until Cabrera got two strikes on him, he was liable to bunt, and Williams did not want the rotund Garces on the mound trying to make a play on the bunt. It was unassailable thinking, but Williams was more worried about not making Garces sound bad than explaining why he made the move.

Also, Williams was resolutely fearless in doing what he thought was right, an example being his philosophy on stolen bases. Under Williams, Red Sox opponents stole a lot of bases, in large part because he did not want his pitchers to use the slide step, a way of speeding up the release of the ball to home plate. The problem with the slide step is that it made pitchers use their arms and shoulders more and increased the risk of injury.

Williams simply would not put his pitchers at risk that way. He also knew that, while it was easy to measure how many stolen bases the opposition had, it wasn't at all possible to measure how many more batters Boston pitchers got out over time because they were concentrating on them, and not picking off the guy at first. So, even though it made him look bad at times, Williams stuck to his guns about holding men on base.

Fans never really warmed to Williams. He was as low-profile as a major Boston sports personality could be. He didn't have to try to escape the spotlight, since he was so dull when it found him that pretty soon people just ignored him. Williams was from California farm country, the Big Valley, and spent winters in Florida doing landscaping work around his home. In Boston, he lived quietly in a hotel during the season and his best friend in the Red Sox organization was equipment manager Joe Cochrane.

So, when Williams chose to respond to Duquette's defense of Everett, it was an unprecedented occurrence.

Essentially, Williams called the GM out for a showdown. Either fire me, or shut up. Specifically, Williams said, "If I were a general manager, I certainly would back the manager. If you can't back the manager, then you probably have to get rid of him. That's what you need to do [replace him] with somebody you can back."

This was Fenway Park's Cuban Missile Crisis, and with Williams daring Duquette to fire him, the general manager pulled back. Public opinion was overwhelming in its support of Williams, who had clearly been wronged by Everett and his apologist, Duquette. There is no way to prove it, but had Williams not come out and openly challenged Duquette, the manager probably would have been fired over the winter. If Williams had known what 2001 would bring, he probably would have welcomed such a move, no matter what he said in public.

Duquette made a splash during the winter by signing Manny Ramirez, who had become one of the game's best hitters during his seasons in Cleveland. The Indians didn't have enough money to keep Ramirez. The Sox signed him to a ridiculous contract that would pay him more than $160 million over eight years.

Boston played much of the year without three of its best players. Garciaparra had surgery in April to repair his right wrist, did not come back until July 29, then shut it down for the season after playing only 21 games. The hit-by-pitch by Alberto Reyes back in September of 1999, which seemed to be about as consequential as a head cold when it happened, turned out to detour what had seemed to be a Hall of Fame career.

Garciaparra had come back in 2000 to hit .372 and win the batting title, but his power had dropped off. He had 120 RBIs in 2002, but his average dropped to .310. Garciaparra would never again be the ultimate combination of average and production, that he had been from 1997 through 1999.

Varitek shattered his right elbow when he dove to catch a foul ball in a game at Fenway on June 7. Pedro Martinez had shoulder problems and made just 18 starts, only three after the All-Star break.

Then there was more Everett. He missed a team bus during spring training and was suspended, but appealed the suspension and won. During the summer, Everett complained of knee problems, but did little in the way of rehab work and was publicly labeled a malingerer by teammate Trot Nixon. When reporters tried to talk to Everett about Nixon's comments, he said he would not comment because the media had made a liar out of Nixon.

This was ridiculous, of course. The day after he initially spoke out, Nixon re-confirmed that he was quoted accurately. The exchange between Everett and the reporters was actually funny. Although it was time for the clubhouse to be closed, and Sox public relations representative Glenn Wilburn was trying to shoo everybody out, Everett would not shut up.

Finally, the Sox erstwhile center fielder ended the conversation by telling his tormenters, "Bye...bye...bye. Toodle-oo," sending all of them immediately to the nearest dictionary to check the correct spelling of "toodle-oo." As the beleaguered Wilburn, who found himself in the unfortunate position of being a good man working for a bad employer, ushered us out the door, I noted that it was Everett who had kept the conversation going, not us. Wilburn snapped back at me and I responded in kind—the sort of harmless verbal skirmish that happens all the time during a typical season—at which time Everett accused me of being a racist, the rationale being that Wilburn was African-American and I wouldn't think of arguing with a white public relations employee.

"You are so out to lunch," I yelled at Everett as the door finally closed, and it mercifully was the last conversation I ever had with the center fielder.

For all of the turmoil, for all of the injuries, Williams had the Red Sox in first place as late as July 21 and had them within 2 ½ games of the top as late as August 7.

Nine days after which, he was fired.

Williams was canned on August 16, a day after the Sox had lost to Seattle, 6-2, to make it six losses in seven games. It was a bad week of baseball, but not a cataclysmic one. The punishment of firing did not seem to fit the crime of having a bad week with a mediocre team.

Members of the news media got to the ballpark unaware of whom Williams' successor would be. The number of possibilities was limited. There was no one in the farm system who remotely resembled big-league managerial material, and the only member of Williams' coaching staff with any sort of experience was third base coach Gene Lamont.

The Red Sox called an afternoon press conference in the Diamond Club room at the corner of Brookline Avenue and Lansdowne Street and there the press corps waited like the audience at the Oscars. Finally, in through the door came Duquette with a uniformed Joe Kerrigan behind him.

Duquette's explanation for firing Williams was a weak one. "It seemed like everybody was just waiting around to see if there would be a change," the general manager said. So, the manager was fired because everyone expected him to be fired—completely circular logic. Duquette also admitted that Kerrigan was not the first choice, Felipe Alou was, but Alou wanted a longer contract than the team was willing to give.

Kerrigan was not an interim manager. In fact, he was given a contract through the end of the 2003 season, a pretty remarkable deal for a man who had never in his life managed a professional baseball game. With the days of Yawkey-Harrington ownership winding down, it seemed as though the administration had gone into a rewards mode. Duquette was given a contract extension in the middle of the season and now Kerrigan, a loyal Duquette soldier for years, was getting this gift. It was like governors handing out judgeships during their final days in office.

Red Sox players simply rolled their eyes at the change. Boston's pitchers did not like Kerrigan all that much. They perceived him as a dogmatic self-promoter, a knowledgeable coach who was well-versed in the use of statistics, but generally used them to justify some pre-conceived notion.

A perfect example was Tim Wakefield, whom Kerrigan had decided was better as a relief pitcher than a starter because he had better stats as a reliever. Of course he had better stats as a reliever. Any good pitcher would have better stats as a reliever than a starter because his opportunities to fail are limited. That didn't mean that a pitcher like Wakefield was more valuable in the bullpen than in the rotation, and subsequent seasons bore that out. Boston's hitters certainly didn't want a pitching coach telling them what to do so they simply ignored the new manager.

The Sox won Kerrigan's first game, 6-4, over the Mariners but it did not take long to sense that he was in over his head. In the sixth, Jose Offerman was thrown out of the game for arguing balls and strikes with plate umpire Wally Bell; Kerrigan never left the dugout to protect his player. Kerrigan also took the closer's job away from Derek Lowe and gave it to Ugueth Urbina without telling Lowe ahead of time, which naturally infuriated Lowe.

Williams left the scene quietly, without talking to reporters or holding a press conference. He didn't return calls and didn't issue any statements. He left town the same way he managed when he was in town, providing more questions than answers.

He was one of those people who are much better one-on-one than in large groups, and anyone covering the team had to find ways to get Williams alone to have a clue as to what was going on in his mind. My favorite time to talk to him was during batting practice. Williams regularly stood near the third base line before games and hit fungos during BP. He would swing and talk, answering questions cryptically, or with raised eyebrows, and occasionally part the curtains to his personality.

The night before he was fired, Williams was on the field and spotted me and Lamont talking over by the fungo circle. He wandered over on his own and reached into his pockets, where he had two "pearls"—baseball lingo for brand new game balls, as yet unsmeared by Lena Blackburne's famous mud. Unsolicited, he tossed one of them to me and told me to keep it, adding, "If anyone wonders, tell them I gave it to you." And he walked into Red Sox history. I have always wondered if he knew then that he was about to be let go.

Almost immediately after the firing it was obvious that Williams was not the problem, he was the solution. The mercifully brief Kerrigan regime was an irretrievable disaster. The final weeks of the

2001 season looked like the Iraqi retreat from Kuwait at the end of the original Gulf War.

Like his predecessor, Kerrigan had problems with Everett and Alcantara. Alcantara had acted up again in July in Pawtucket, where he had played himself onto the International League All-Star team, then was thrown off of it when he karate-kicked an opposing catcher in the face mask because he thought he had been thrown at.

When Alcantara was called up for September, he played in a game at Yankee Stadium on September 9 and came up to bat in the fourth inning. Alcantara hit a foul pop-up that New York catcher Jorge Posada caught in fair ground; Alcantara never bothered to leave the batter's box to run to first and was taken out of the game by Kerrigan.

That game, a 7-2 loss, made Boston's record 7-16 since Kerrigan had taken over as manager, not exactly what Duquette had expected when he dismissed Williams. It was also the final game the Sox played for ten days, and when they resumed the schedule, the world had changed forever.

Boston was supposed to play the Yankees again on September 10, but the game was rained out, and that night, the Sox headed to their next stop on the road, Tampa Bay. Most of the press contingent stayed in town and five of us—myself, Gordon Edes of the *Boston Globe*, Sean McAdam of the *Providence Journal*, and Tony Massarotti and Jeff Horrigan of the *Boston Herald*—had an early flight out of LaGuardia Airport on the morning of September 11.

It was a perfect September morning and Manhattan never looked more stunning as our plane banked to the left and headed south for Tampa. We turned out to be among the last people ever to see New York as it appeared on the post cards. Less than a half hour after we flew over the Hudson River, the first plane hit the World Trade Center.

We were probably over North Carolina when our plane's pilot came on the intercom and began to explain what was going on north of us in New York and Washington, D.C. There was no sense of fear or panic in his voice as he told us that we had to get out of the sky as quickly as possible, and would be landing shortly in Atlanta.

On the ground, we exited the plane quickly and quietly. The airport was full of bewildered travelers, much as we were, but again it was an orderly, calm, rational scene. Our airline, American, had found rooms for us at a Holiday Inn in nearby Jonesboro, Georgia, but could not provide transportation there. After we got out luggage, we flagged down a commercial van and with sufficient financial inducement, got the driver to take us to Jonesboro.

At that point, there was little we could do but wait. The games scheduled for Tampa had been called off with no word on when play would resume. We hung around Jonesboro for two nights, then decided to try and make our way back north. If the Sox were going to play again, their first games would be in Baltimore. McAdam was able to locate a van we could rent, and we headed out of town, bound for Maryland.

As night fell, we were in South Carolina, and practically all the way through the original hotbed of secession. Massarotti was driving and about a mile from the North Carolina state line, we were pulled over by a South Carolina state trooper. It was Smokey and the Bandit law enforcement in real life. Massarotti got a ticket for doing 60 in a 55 mph zone.

We spent the night in North Carolina, then arrived in Baltimore just as the announcement was made that those games were postponed, too. We stopped at the Marriott in downtown Baltimore and were allowed to file stories from there. After that, it was time to go home. We drove up the New Jersey Turnpike in the dead of night and as we neared Newark, could look off to the east and see the ruins of the World Trade Center, still smoldering under the blinding glare of spotlights.

While we were making our way home in a van, the Red Sox were on a northbound train. We were able to talk with Kerrigan via the phone, but got few details beyond the fact that the team was on a train. When asked where, Kerrigan replied, "We can't state publicly our intentions, or where we're going to work out." This was typical disconnected-from-reality Red Sox paranoia. With downtown Manhattan still shrouded in smoke and the walls of the Pentagon breached, the Sox figured that if terrorists really wanted to destroy the nation's will, they would attack the team train as it headed for Boston.

Play resumed on September 19, but before that teams had a couple of days of practice—mini-camps in essence—to prepare. All of the mini-camps were to be open to the news media, per order of the Commissioner of Baseball, but the Red Sox defied the order and kept their practice sessions closed. Perhaps it was just more of their over-inflated sense of self-importance and they sincerely believed that Fenway Park was on the short list of Al-Queda targets. Or, more likely, they simply did not want anyone to see how badly things had deteriorated under Kerrigan.

People found out, anyway, or at least Jeff Horrigan of the *Boston Herald* did. He wrote a story saying that on the Sunday before play resumed, Everett was late for practice. When he arrived, Kerrigan told him he would be fined. Everett unleashed some more unrestrained venom in the direction of the manager, following him out of the clubhouse and down into the dugout, screaming all the way.

The center fielder was fined and suspended for four games. He never played another game in a Red Sox uniform.

The season hit rock bottom in Tampa Bay on the first two days of October when Boston lost back to back games to the Devil Rays by 10-3 scores. The Red Sox had been 16 games over .500 on June 12 at 43-27 and had fallen to two games below, 77-79, under Kerrigan, whose record at that point was 12-26. However, Boston rallied to win its final five games of the season and at least finish in the black.

The final game of the season was in Baltimore on October 6. Boston won it, 5-1, behind strong pitching by David Cone. It was the final game played under the long and spectacularly unsuccessful

Yawkey-Harrington ownership, a reign of error that had lasted 68 years. Both Kerrigan and Duquette, contract extensions or not, had also seen their last games as Red Sox employees.

With them gone, and with new ownership in place, when the 2002 season opened, the end of the tunnel would finally be visible to Red Sox fans. And the light at the end of it was no longer light years away. Precisely how close it was, though, no one could have imagined.

# SNAPSHOT

## The Crankiest Man in Baseball

There is a Gold Standard in every profession. Novelists are compared to Hemingway, singers to Sinatra, businessmen to Rockefeller. The Gold Standard for grouchiness was set by Red Sox infielder Mike Lansing.

Boston acquired Lansing in a trading deadline deal with the Rockies in July of 2000. He arrived along with Rolando Arrojo and Rich Croushore. Colorado got Brian Rose, John Wasdin, Jeff Frye and minor leaguer Jeff Taglienti. It was the perfect trade in that neither team benefited from it.

Lansing was from Casper, Wyoming, not the most fertile ground to develop baseball players, and maybe it was the long winters, or the four-hour drives to the next town, but somewhere along the line he had turned into the world's crankiest person.

It was an interesting crankiness, though. Lansing would snarl, bark and snap when someone tried to talk with him, but would always talk, and usually respond with rational, intelligent answers. But the process of trying to deal with him was almost unbearable at times.

Once, as reporters stood outside of manager Jimy Williams' door, waiting for him to invite us in for the daily pre-game conference, Lansing took exception to the fact that some of us were watching the clubhouse TV and yelled at Boston BaseBall Writers Association chapter chairman Sean McAdam.

"What do you want us to do—look at the floor?" was McAdam's reply and that was enough to satisfy Lansing, who returned to sullen silence.

Another time, in a misguided attempt to pry some humanity out of him, I mentioned that in a cross-country trip, my wife and I had driven through Casper, and right past the place where that city's Class A minor league team plays—Mike Lansing Field.

Casper was also where Tom Browning and Mike Devereaux played high school baseball, so having a field named after him sort of set Lansing apart, it seemed. I asked him about visiting the ballpark named after him.

"Why the [deuce] would I want to do that?" Lansing responded. "You know, I'm kind of busy during the baseball season, and in the winter, it's kind of snowy up in Casper, so why would I go there? I'll get there one day, I'm sure."

So much for thinking that someone would actually be honored to visit a baseball park named after him while he was still alive.

The worst Lansing moment happened in New York.

The Red Sox had flown into the city very early on the morning of June 4, 2001, to play a makeup game against the

Yankees, after finishing a four-game series in Toronto. The Sox were staying at the Grand Hyatt Hotel at Grand Central Station, and during the evening, one baseball-fan dad had found out from a bellman that the team was due to arrive after midnight.

So the dad was in the hotel lobby in the wee hours, with his young son, when the Sox checked in and filed up to their rooms. They were nice people—no autograph seeking, no picture-taking, just a chance to see the Red Sox in street clothes—but when Lansing saw them, he went off.

What's wrong with you, he shouted at the father, getting a kid out of bed at this hour of the night just to look at some baseball players? It was the old "get a life" monologue, and the other Sox who saw it were horrified to think that anyone would act that way to fans who could not have been more respectful. For some, it was as embarrassed they had ever felt as baseball players.

For much of the 2001 season, when Nomar Garciaparra was recovering from wrist surgery, Lansing was Boston's starting shortstop. He did a good job, too, but nobody was sorry to see him go when his Sox career ended that year.

# Deliverance at Last

UNLIKE INTERIM GENERAL MANAGER MIKE PORT, GRADY LITTLE did not have the "interim" in his title. Nevertheless, he was interim too, just interim with a longer leash.

He got off to a fabulous start thanks to the starting pitching of Martinez and Lowe, both of whom finished the season as 20-game winners. Lowe pitched a no-hitter against the Devil Rays at Fenway Park on April 27, 2002, the first no-hitter in Boston since Dave Morehead's in September of 1965, the day that Mike Higgins was fired as general manager. Port survived this one.

Varitek, Garciaparra and Martinez had come back from their 2001 injury problems to re-establish themselves as regulars, but only Varitek was what you would call the same player. Garciaparra was clearly not the hitter he once was and while Martinez still overwhelmed the competition on most days, he had changed his style, and threw his fastball less often. Freed from the constraints put on him by Kerrigan, Tim Wakefield resurrected his career as a starter under Little and new pitching coach Tony Cloninger and had his best season in years.

The opening day roster included outfielders Johnny Damon and Rickey Henderson. The Sox hoped that Damon was in his prime.

Henderson was clearly past his, but remained in exquisite physical condition and had played on a lot of winning teams during his long career. Boston hoped that he could be a solid spare outfielder and transfer some of that championship experience to his teammates, even if only by osmosis.

Damon had been an excellent player with the Royals, but spent 2001 in Oakland and had the worst season of his career as he faced his first shot at free agency. Boston gambled that the security of the four-year contract it gave him would allow Damon to be the same player he was in Kansas City, and the Sox turned out to be right.

Henderson was Henderson—outspoken, funny, eccentric, unpredictable. He came to the organization on a minor-league contract and early on, as he and the Sox tried to agree on a big-league deal, Henderson updated, so to speak, how the negotiations were going.

"Have you signed your contract?" he was asked during a informal press conference.

"Have I read my contract?" Henderson responded.

"No. Have you signed your contract?" was the response, to which Henderson replied, "Now, why would I sign something I haven't read?"

End of press conference.

In May of that year, with Boston playing at Tampa Bay, Henderson was in left field. At Tropicana Field, the dreary dome that the Devil Rays call home, the seats in the left-field corner come up almost to the foul line. On this night, a family sat in the front row, enjoying the view, when a high fly headed in their direction. The mother grabbed her baby to protect her from the fly ball, and Henderson was able to reach up and make the catch in foul ground. Standing just inches away from the mother and baby, Henderson leaned over, kissed the baby on the forehead like a presidential candidate, smiled and trotted in to the Boston dugout.

The pieces all fit together very nicely at first. On June 20, the Red Sox were 45-24 and on top of the AL East standings. After that,

Boston did not collapse, it just slowly faded, first out of the league lead, then out of wild card contention.

On September 9 in Tampa Bay, in the third inning of a game versus the Devil Rays, Ramirez hit a one-hopper back to Tampa pitcher Tanyon Sturtze. Ramirez turned and headed for the dugout without heading towards first base, setting a record in the process. By the time Sturtze threw the ball to first, Ramirez was 15 feet towards the bench, becoming the first player to be out at first by 105 feet.

Little left Ramirez in the game, and he homered as part of a 6-3 victory. The next day Little told reporters that he had made a mistake and should have taken him out right then and there. Rather then turn into some kind of divisive issue, the Ramirez controversy sparked a Red Sox resurgence. They went on a 12-4 run to fight off elimination for a while, but even that surge wasn't enough.

Boston lost in Chicago, 7-2, on September 25, to end any hope of making the playoffs. When Carlos Baerga tapped back to the pitcher for the final out Port, sitting quietly in the back row of the press box, hung his head and looked at the counter top for a few seconds before making his way down to the clubhouse. Although it would not be official for some time, Port would never be more than the interim general manager, and he knew it.

Theo Epstein was one month shy of his 29th birthday when named general manager on November 25, 2002. He went into the free-agent market and signed oft-injured infielder Bill Mueller, and former Twins first baseman David Ortiz, a frightening physical presence at the plate who had never really blossomed in Minnesota. Epstein made a convoluted deal to get utility man Kevin Millar, who had seemed headed to Japan, and traded for second baseman Todd Walker, a solid hitter with a reputation as a limited player defensively.

The Sox' bullpen was awful, and in May Epstein traded third baseman Shea Hillenbrand to Arizona for reliever B.K. Kim. It turned out to be a lousy trade—Kim was best remembered for giving Fenway fans the middle finger during playoff introductions in

2003, and having to call the Fort Myers police when he was locked in after taking a nap in the owner's box at City of Palms Park at spring training, 2004—but it was a sign that Epstein recognized the value of pitching and was not afraid to gamble. Lowe was not as good in 2003 as he was in 2002 and Martinez won just 14 games, although the bullpen blew five saves behind him.

The problem was that Martinez used to be his own best closer and pitch eight innings and sometimes nine. He had become almost brittle and left games earlier than in his prime; injuries and illnesses held him to just 29 starts for the season, and he looked tired by September.

Still, with Ortiz having a breakthrough season and Millar providing a great deal of energy as well as some timely power, the Red Sox made the playoffs. Walker proved to be an excellent pickup. He hit well in the clutch and was a better fielder than advertised. Mueller stunned the baseball world by becoming one of the least likely batting champions in history, barely edging out teammate Ramirez. The season ended with a meaningless game in Tampa, after which Mueller was officially crowned batting champion.

Sitting in front of his locker accepting congratulations, a lonely bottle of champagne sitting in a bucket of ice next to him, Mueller seemed almost bored with the entire experience, but this was his personality. Back on July 29 in Texas, he had become the first player in the history of baseball to hit grand slams from different sides of the plate in the same game and reacted with underwhelming emotion that time, too.

As the season went on, it increasingly belonged to Ortiz.

A huge man, physically, Ortiz had an equally imposing personality. But unlike so many newcomers who had brought smiles into the Boston clubhouse when they arrived, then hardened in the oppressive atmosphere, Ortiz was irrepressible. It was a matter of right place, right time. The new ownership no longer discouraged happy players.

The Red Sox were Ortiz' third organization. He had been signed by the Mariners, and they essentially gave him to the Twins in a trade for washed-up veteran Dave Hollins. Minnesota should have been perfect for Ortiz with its short fence in right, but the best he could do was hit 20 home runs in 2002. The Twins finally grew tired of waiting around for him to grow up as a player, and when they did, the Sox got him cheap as sort of a left-handed complement to Millar.

In Boston, it took a while for Ortiz to get going. In his debut game, he went 0 for 6. In April, he hit just one home run, although it turned out to be an indicator of what was to come. The homer was in Anaheim on April 22, in the 14th inning, breaking a 4-4 tie in a game Boston eventually won, 6-4. By June 1, Ortiz had hit just two homers, and by July 2 had only four. To that point in the season, Ortiz in Boston was not much different than the Minnesota experience, but that changed quickly, and dramatically.

He homered in a game in Tampa Bay on July 3, then went north with the Sox to Yankee Stadium where he homered twice on July 4 and twice again on July 5. Now, there was no way to keep Ortiz out of the lineup and he never stopped producing. In a stretch of nine games from August 23 to 30, Ortiz hit seven home runs.

Still, as September arrived, the Sox were in trouble. They lost to the Yankees on August 31, 8-4, and were 5 ½ games out of first place, and 1 ½ games behind the Mariners in the wild-card race. Boston began September with a long road trip made even longer by the fact that it had to play one game in Philadelphia as a makeup of a postponement. That game was on September 1 and for eight innings, it was as ugly as baseball gets.

The Sox used five pitchers, the Phillies seven. There were errors and baserunning blunders. Both teams blew leads. Boston was up, 7-6, going into the bottom of the eighth but the bullpen gave up three runs and the Sox trailed by two as they came up in the top of the ninth.

Boston loaded the bases with one out, scored a run on Lou Merloni's infield hit, then tied it when Phillies reliever Turk Wendel walked Millar with the bases-loaded. That brought up Nixon, who took Ball One, then sent Wendell's second pitch over the right-field fence for a grand slam. Kim came on and closed out the 13-9 victory in the ninth and the Sox were off on a tear.

They went to Chicago and beat the White Sox on September 2. On September 3, they trailed the White Sox in the eighth, 3-2, when Ortiz' two-run homer made it 4-3. Chicago came back to make it 4-4 in the last of the eighth, but no matter. Ortiz homered again in the 10th and Boston had a 5-4 victory. Starting with that game in Philadelphia, the Sox won 15 of 21 games and set themselves up for the playoffs.

Boston clinched a wild-card berth by beating the Orioles at Fenway Park on September 25. The final out set off a crazy, over-the-top celebration. As the players cavorted like madmen on the field, with some 35,000 fans screaming from the stands, John Henry wandered around in front of the Red Sox dugout looking dazed. Until now, he knew of the emotions created by his team only in an abstract sense. This was reality, and it could be scary.

In its first visit to the playoffs since 1999, Boston played Oakland, with the Athletics having home field for three of the five games. The first two were played in Oakland and the A's won them both, sending the series back to Fenway Park for Game 3 on October 4 with the Sox a loss away from elimination. What ensued was one of the most confusing and illogical post-season games ever played, the kind of game Red Sox teams had often played in the past, and usually lost.

Not this time, though.

It was 1-0, Red Sox, in the sixth when Oakland appeared to have scored three times, but got just one run. The first play happened when Eric Byrnes tried to score from third on a ground ball; Varitek blocked the plate—probably illegally but he was the best in the business at doing the premature block and not getting called for it—and

Byrnes not only missed tagging home, but got hurt in the process. Varitek tagged him out behind the plate.

Two batters later, Garciaparra made an error at shortstop on a ground ball by Ramon Hernandez, with Erubiel Durazo scoring from third to tie it. On the play, Miguel Tejada, running from second base, collided with Sox third baseman Bill Mueller. Mueller was immediately called for interference, which Tejada took to mean that he was awarded home.

But it did not. Since the interference happened before Tejada reached third, that base was all he was entitled to. When he kept going for home, he was on his own and was tagged out in the middle of the baseline. That out ended the inning, and the score was just 1-1.

It remained that way into the last of the 11th when, with one out, Doug Mirabelli singled and Trot Nixon came up to pinch-hit for Gabe Kapler. Nixon homered into the center field bleachers, the first game-ending homer in the post-season for Boston since Carlton Fisk's Game 6 blast in 1975, and the Red Sox had a 3-1 victory, and some life.

They ran with it, winning the next night at Fenway, then taking the series with a 4-3 victory in Oakland on Monday, October 6, a win that came with a price. In the seventh inning, Damon came in on a shallow fly ball hit by Jermaine Dye. As he came in, second baseman Damian Jackson went out. The two collided, with Damon winding up on the ground, unconscious. He had to leave the game with what was later diagnosed as a concussion.

The Division Series victory over the A's sent the Sox into the ALCS, once again versus the Yankees, and once again with New York having four games at home. The teams split the first two games at Yankee Stadium, then came to Fenway Park for Game 3 on Saturday, October 11. It was 2-2 heading into the top of the fourth, with Pedro Martinez pitching for the Sox and Roger Clemens for the Yankees.

In the top of the fourth, Martinez walked Jorge Posada, then gave up a single to Nick Johnson and a double to Hideki Matsui, New York taking a 3-2 lead. That brought up Yankees' right fielder Karim Garcia, whom Martinez hit with a pitch, inciting another Sox-Yanks Armageddon. By the time the bottom of the fourth was over, both benches had cleared and Yankees bench coach Don Zimmer was lying on the dirt in front of the Boston dugout.

After Ramirez had over-reacted to a high pitch thrown by Clemens, Zimmer went charging at Martinez. Zimmer had managed the Sox during their 1978 collapse, one of the bitterest, most over-sized pills any Red Sox fan ever swallowed. Pitcher Bill Lee had called Zimmer a gerbil, and that nickname had stuck, although the passage of time had healed the worst of the wounds. Zimmer had actually briefly been back as a Red Sox coach under Butch Hobson, and these days, fans viewed him as an artifact, sort of the Sox' version of Herbert Hoover in semi-retirement.

Zimmer was 72, and as he neared Martinez, the pitcher faced the ultimate lose-lose dilemma. He could let the old man knock him down and forever be known as the major-league baseball player who got pushed over by a senior citizen, or he could knock Zimmer down and forever be known as the major-league baseball player who pushed over a senior citizen.

Martinez chose the latter. *Boston Herald* reporter Michael Silverman referred to Zimmer as the "Raging Gerbil" and the next day, the Yankees' coach apologized for his actions in a brief news conference that ended prematurely when he broke down in tears.

But the Zimmer-Martinez confrontation was just Act 1. Between the top and bottom of the ninth inning, a fight broke out in the Yankees bullpen between Sox employee Paul Williams and New York reliever Jeff Nelson. Nelson was a notorious hothead and Williams, a member of the grounds crew, had been openly rooting for Boston as the game progressed. Garcia jumped the bullpen fence to join the battle. He and Williams both wound up with minor injuries before things were broken up.

After which, Mariano Rivera set Boston down in order to preserve a 4-3 Yankees victory.

The teams went to New York with the Yankees leading the series, 3 games to 2. Damon had returned to the lineup, probably prematurely. In a contact sport like hockey, the protocol for even a mild concussion is a minimum of two weeks off from any sort of strenuous activity. Damon's concussion was severe, but he was back in a matter of days.

The Red Sox won Game 6, 9-6, to set up the ultimate baseball showdown, a Red Sox-Yankees Game 7. It was not the first winner-take-all game between the teams. The last game of the 1949 season at Yankee Stadium was such a game, and New York won it. The 1978 playoff at Fenway Park was such a game, and New York won it.

And the Yankees won this one, as well, coming back from a 4-0 deficit to do it. The starters were Martinez and Clemens, and the Rocket Man clearly did not have it; the game was won when New York manager Joe Torre gave Clemens a quick hook in the top of the fourth.

Millar led the inning with a homer. Nixon walked, then Bill Mueller singled him to third. The Red Sox had a 4-0 lead with men at first and third and none out when Torre replaced Clemens with Mussina. The Yankees were about to crack, and the crowd of 55,000 or so watched silently with a collective sense of doom. Jason Varitek was the first batter to face Mussina, and he struck out. Damon was up next and he hit a sizzling grounder to shortstop Derek Jeter, who started an inning-ending double play.

It was a last-second phone call from the governor. The Yankees were reprieved and they took advantage of their second life.

Months later, Damon was asked about how much the concussion affected him during the Yankees series, and more specifically about him hitting into a double play in the fourth inning. It made a difference, Damon admitted. Had he not felt a little "fuzzy," he would have gotten around faster on that pitch from Mussina, maybe hit it up the middle for a single, maybe pulled it towards right field where at the very least it would not have been a double play ball.

Little's career as Red Sox manager ended in the bottom of the eighth when New York scored three runs to forge a 5-5 tie. Martinez was still in the game and got the first out of the inning, then gave up four straight hits—a double to Jeter, a single by Bernie Williams, a double to Matsui and finally a two-run bloop double by Posada that tied the game.

Little lifted Martinez after Posada's double, but it was too late. The game was lost there, just as Game 6 of the 1986 World Series was lost when the Mets tied it on Bob Stanley's wild pitch. Baseball games take on lives of their own, and this Game 7 had been willed to the Yankees, who won it on Aaron Boone's home run off of Tim Wakefield in the 11th.

Did Little deserve to be fired for leaving Martinez in? Of course he did. It was a mistake too big to be overlooked or ignored. Nothing he had done as Red Sox manager after that, short of going 162-0 and winning a World Series, would have made people forget.

If Posada had hit the ball 300 feet instead of 200, the Red Sox would probably have won the game, but that kind of play is what makes baseball unique. It is an unfair, illogical game, which is why Little should have lifted Martinez sooner, rather than later.

The manager had to change the direction of the inning, as Torre had changed the direction of the fourth when he removed Clemens.

Fans of a certain age can think back to one of the great innings in Red Sox history, the sixth inning of their game with the Twins on the final day of the 1967 season. That inning started with a Jim Lonborg bunt. Jerry Adair followed with a ground ball single that would have been a double play had it been hit five feet to the left or right. Dalton Jones followed with another seeing-eye grounder for a hit to load the bases. Carl Yastrzemski had a legit single to center, but the Sox scored more runs on errors and wild pitches.

The inning that gave them the 1967 pennant made no sense at all. It was grunge baseball.

Just as Posada's double was a grunge hit. Maybe it could not have been prevented, but changing pitchers would have made it less likely.

Epstein didn't waste any time changing managers after the Marlins had finished beating the Yankees in the World Series. He hired Terry Francona, who had once managed the Phillies for four gloriously unsuccessful seasons from 1997 to 2000, but had resurrected himself as a candidate with bench coach stints in Texas and Oakland.

Francona was introduced at a press conference in the .406 Club at Fenway and immediately gave off the impression that he had no idea what he was getting into. He was far too friendly, far too accommodating, far too optimistic. In the case of a miserable old troll like McNamara, it was fun watching the job of Red Sox manager destroy him. Watching Francona get chewed up would not be fun.

Epstein did more than change managers in the wake of 2003's ALCS trauma. He added a great starting pitcher in Curt Schilling, whom Francona knew from Philadelphia; and a great reliever in Keith Foulke, whom Francona knew from Oakland.

Schilling was what people liked to call a "presence." He had opinions, and he liked being on camera. Long ago, the Sox had traded him to Baltimore in the Mike Boddicker deal. Since then, Schilling had learned his craft and was undeniably one of the best in the game. He was also more than a little self-important, as he demonstrated when he arrived in Fort Myers for spring training.

Rather than do 20 separate interviews, he suggested a group session, which was a perfectly reasonable way to handle things. Schilling set the time, 12:15, and the place—the picnic tables outside of the minor-league clubhouse, the same spot where John Henry and Larry Lucchino had camped out in 2002 waiting for the sale of the club to be finalized. By 12:15, the media throng had assembled in wait.

Schilling finally came out at 3 P.M.

In terms of performance, such things were irrelevant. Schilling was a great pitcher and had a great season. Foulke was excellent, too. Francona was the ultimate players' manager, rarely being critical, almost always finding some positive in the most distressing of performances. Which was perfect for a veteran team like the Red Sox, who really needed a lifeguard more than a manager, and Francona knew just when he had to go into the water.

By the end of July, the tide was out. Garciaparra and Nixon both got hurt in spring training; Boston's shortstop through some of the season's first half was Cesar Crespo, who distinguished himself by coming up to bat 79 times without ever once drawing a walk.

Garciaparra's relationship with the fans had remained strong as injuries reduced his effectiveness, but by 2004 he had entered into a Cold War with the news media in general. He had the team create a red line in the clubhouse carpet beyond which no media member could step. This was completely unenforceable by the rules of access and was laughable, but a symptom of his increasing discomfort with the spotlight.

Early in spring training of 2004, Garciaparra tried to mend fences. He asked a few of the regular beat reporters to talk with him about rebuilding the relationship and that sounded like a good idea. Instead, a horde of reporters descended upon him at the appointed time—exactly the sort of thing he detested—and nothing got fixed.

Meanwhile, in Fort Myers, Garciaparra hurt his right Achilles tendon in a batting practice accident that no one saw. He did not play a regulation game until June 9 and upon his return, hit well for average, but had no power. Even worse, he had no range at shortstop and had gone from being the best infielder on the team to a liability. Increasingly morose and distant, as the summer wore on,

Garciaparra began to take on the appearance of man put on death row for a crime he didn't commit. "Get me out of here" said the expression on his face, and on July 31 in Minneapolis, Epstein obliged him.

The trade came literally at the last minute and was part of a very complex deal involving several teams and players. As Garciaparra departed the Sox clubhouse in the Metrodome, he stopped to speak with reporters. To the end, he tried hard to do the right thing. After the questions stopped, he shook everybody's hand and wished them well. In fact, he kept shaking hands even after completing the circle, doing some a second time.

When he finally realized that he was shaking some hands a second time, he said sheepishly, "I wanted to thank everybody. And some people more than once" before heading down the hall for Chicago.

The trade, which brought Orlando Cabrera in to replace Garciaparra at shortstop, and added Doug Mientkiewicz and Dave Roberts, saved the season. It took the Sox a few games to re-organize, but after they did, they were the best team in the league and roared into the playoffs as a Wild Card team once again.

The franchise and its fans had been down that road before and knew how it ended. Logic says that nothing lasts forever, even disappointment, but the Red Sox had never let logic guide their fate.

This time was different, finally. Boston swept the Angels in the Division Series, Ortiz winning the third game with a sudden-death home run. The Sox followed that up with the greatest come-from-behind story in sports history, beating the Yankees in four straight after losing the first three games. Game 7 was in Yankee Stadium again, but this one belonged to Boston from the first pitch to the last. Francona, who had refused to bench Damon and the slumping Mark Bellhorn when they were useless early in the series, was magnificent in holding things together.

Schilling had hurt his right ankle in the Anaheim series and was ineffective in Game One of the ALCS. He had the ankle fixed by team doctor Bill Morgan in an unprecedented procedure and responded with two superb starts.

The Cardinals never had a chance in the World Series. The Red Sox never trailed throughout the four-game sweep. It had taken John Henry and his partners less than three calendar years to wipe away the 68-year stain of Yawkey ownership.

Deliverance was at hand.

# SNAPSHOT

## Manny Being Manny

Monday, October 4, 2004 was a typically warm and sunny day in Southern California, and late that afternoon the Red Sox were scheduled to meet at Angels Stadium for a workout the day before their Division Series with the Angels began.

The parking lot surrounding the ballpark was busy with curious fans, prospective ticket purchasers, Angels employees and members of the news media heading in for the workout.

I was one of the media members, and as I walked the perimeter of the stadium seeking the right entrance, was hailed by Manny Ramirez, who was strolling through the buzzing crowd unnoticed and oblivious. "Hey, man"— Ramirez did not know many names and tended to call all familiar faces "man"—"How do I get inside?" he asked me.

"That's what I'm trying to find out," I answered. "Follow me. We'll find it." And we did, in fairly short order. I signed in for credentials and headed for the press box. Ramirez was waved through to the Red Sox clubhouse, where he had a date with baseball history.

He arrived in Boston in 2001 and hit a three-run homer in his first Fenway at bat in a Red Sox uniform. General manager Dan Duquette overpaid for Ramirez, which was OK with the Harrington ownership because they knew somebody else would be writing the checks come 2002, and because of the money, Boston was stuck with the inscrutable left fielder no matter how badly either side might have wanted a divorce.

Ramirez quickly became one of the most maddening players ever to wear a Red Sox uniform. There was no doubting his magnificent offensive skills, but he often floated through the season like an abandoned fishing boat with no apparent direction or destination in sight.

The annual question was—were the Red Sox better with him, or without him? Some good players had preceded Ramirez onto the horns of that dilemma, the first being Babe Ruth. By the end of the 1919 season, the Red Sox had tired of Ruth's demands for special treatment, occasional lackadaisical play, his disregard for his teammates and disrespect for management, and sold him to the Yankees.

Were the Red Sox better with, or without, Ruth?

In the early 1950s, after Boston had stopped being a contender, and before he had taken on mystical status, Ted Williams had to deal with the "with or without" question, also. Tom Yawkey decided "with" and for the last five years of his career, Williams provided the only reason for baseball fans to come to Fenway Park.

Baseball is a uniquely individual team sport, and those who

play it are very forgiving of its eccentric stars, for they know that in the long run, the stars make everybody richer. And so Ramirez' Red Sox teammates were forgiving of him. They saw the special treatment, and understood that a) he was not malicious, only disconnected from reality and, b) without him, there would be no post-season for them.

Since Ramirez rarely spoke with reporters—other than the occasional "Hey, man"—he was often portrayed as unfriendly, or arrogant, neither of which were true. He just didn't want to be bothered. In spring training of 2004, Kevin Millar made an effort to have Ramirez talk more for the record, starting with an impromptu press conference during which Millar acted as Master of Ceremonies and translator.

It was a good show, and earned Ramirez some brownie points all-around, but in the end, it was nothing more than theater. When Ramirez did talk to reporters, he said absolutely nothing. Nobody ever walked away from a conversation with the slugger having even the tiniest insight into what was going on inside of him.

He drove managers crazy, and opposing pitchers even crazier. Manny Ramirez—were the Red Sox better with him or without him? Harry Frazee would have been able to answer that question.

# Epilogue:
# Game 4, 2004 World Series

BEFORE THE CARDINALS CAME UP TO BAT IN THE BOTTOM OF THE ninth inning, I got up from my seat in the press box to stretch my legs. At the same time, Tony Massarotti of the *Boston Herald* had the same idea, and he walked over to where I was standing and asked, "Did you ever think you'd live to see this day?"

In the *Telegram & Gazette*'s annual pre-season picks, I had predicted the Red Sox would win the World Series, so from a professional standpoint yes, I had figured to live the seven months between the end of spring training and the World Series.

From the standpoint of having spent all of my previous 52 years living in New England, though, watching the Red Sox warm up for the last of the ninth was like watching the fuzzy, grainy, black-and-white TV images of Neil Armstrong stepping onto the moon.

Was it real?

Ever since the laptop replaced the typewriter as a journalist's doodle pad of choice, press boxes have been fairly quiet places. On this night, the front row of the Busch Stadium press box was populated by some of the best in the business—my colleague, Phil O'Neill, directly to my right; then the *Hartford Courant*'s Dave

Heuschkel and columnist Jeff Jacobs. Directly to my left were Bob Hohler and Dan Shaughnessy of the *Boston Globe*; Jeff Horrigan and Massarotti of the *Herald* were on that side of the press box, too, along with Sean McAdam and Steve Krasner of the *Providence Journal*.

No one had written more, or more skillfully, about the failures of the Red Sox than Shaughnessy. While legions of Sox fans would have loved to believe that Shaughnessy had watched Game 4 as if his life were passing before his eyes, in fact he spent the night like all of us, tapping away at the keyboard, searching for perspective, trying to find the right words to describe the indescribable.

Papers throughout New England including the *Telegram & Gazette* had pushed back their deadlines so as to get Game 4 into as many editions as possible. So I had written a bare-bones story along the way and prepared to top it off with something about the Sox' impending victory. Baseball writers don't have the luxury of worrying about jinxes and the like, and pure logic said that Boston would win this game, and the World Series.

My wife, Debbie, was in St. Louis with me for the series, although not at the games. I had decided that I would call her from the stadium, for the final outs, and was getting ready to dial when Albert Pujols bounced a single through Keith Foulke's legs and into center field.

Hold the phone.

But Foulke quickly got Scott Rolen to fly out to right, and when Jim Edmonds came to bat, I started to dial again. Edmonds went out on three strikes and my wife answered her cell phone just as Edgar Renteria took Ball One.

Debbie had sat with me, being microwaved, through a hot Memorial Day doubleheader at Fenway Park in 1971, one in which the Sox were swept by the Royals, and had married me on the day that Boston and Cincinnati played Game One of the 1975 World Series. She had celebrated three times in 1986—when the Sox clinched the AL East title, when they won Game 5 in Anaheim, and when they won Game 7 at Fenway—and had had her heart torn out twice in the World Series.

"I wanted you to be able to hear. . ." I began to say, and then Renteria hit a one-hopper back to Foulke. There was silence as he ran towards Doug Mientkiewicz, then flipped the ball to him for the final out of the game. Then I said, "My God—the Red Sox just won the World Series. I have to write."

Generally, when the final out of a game is made, the press box empties as if somebody had just called in a bomb threat. But this was different. We all sat silently, taking in the scene, understanding that this was like being in the room at Appomattox when Robert E. Lee surrendered the Army of Northern Virginia.

With a minute or two to spare before I went down to the club-house, I called my oldest daughter, Abby, in Chicago, where I knew she and her boyfriend, Chuck Brinkman, were watching the game together. What a confluence of baseball misery that was. Chuck was a lifelong White Sox fan and had worked as an usher at Comiskey Park. Together, he and Abby were fans of teams that had not won a World Series in 175 seasons.

Until this minute.

It was not much of a conversation. Abby, a graduate of the University of Chicago, was completely incoherent. She made sounds, but they were not words. I said a quick goodbye, and then really did have to go to work.

Later, after I had filed my final story, I packed up my computer bag and walked down into the seats, hopped a rail and went onto the field where some of the Sox players had returned to celebrate with their families and friends. As I took in the scene, I thought of my friend Steve Tripoli, now of Sudbury, but who was in Beijing, China in 1986 and had to listen to the agonies of Games 6 and 7 via short-wave radio, the signal fading in and out, and who was so distraught that he literally could not speak to his co-workers for several hours after returning from lunch—it being lunchtime on the other side of the world when Game 6 ended.

Later, Steve told me that when Renteria made the final out, he unconsciously dropped to his knees in a combination of wonderment and disbelief.

I thought of John Bart in Easthampton, whose Red Sox memories went back to Walt Dropo and Clyde Vollmer and Billy Consolo, and who was still playing baseball in a men's league when he was in his 50s. John was the managing editor at my first paper, the *Amherst Record*, and had kept in touch on a frequent basis during the years I covered the Sox. In the spring, I had told him for the first time ever that I thought Boston would win the World Series. He was stunned and delighted and kept up a steady correspondence through the summer.

John was also, in the summer of 2004, gravely ill with cancer, and I heard from him less and less frequently. The day after Game 4, though, there was email in my box from him, wanting to know just how it could have happened that the Red Sox won the World Series.

I wrote back that it was a combination of things—better ownership, better players, and all of the bad luck that Boston had been plagued with in the past fusing into an atomic explosion of good fortune over a span of seven glorious games.

"Just as I thought," he wrote back in what was his last email. John Bart died less than a month after Game 4.

I have never done the autograph thing, but keep odd mementoes from games and seasons past. I had both Young and Flaherty sign my scorebook from the Cleveland no-hitter, for instance, but never went much beyond that sort of souvenir. However, the 2004 post-season was a bit different. From the point where Ortiz' home run won Game 4 of the ALCS, it seemed as though something historic might be underway, and I tucked away credentials, programs, even the security tags we got on our computer bags when reporting to the ballpark every afternoon.

For the League Championship Series, and World Series, Major League Baseball provides reporters with box lunches—chips, an apple, a soda, some cookies and a sandwich. So it was in New York for Game 7 of the ALCS, but the night was so busy that I never got to eat my sandwich. I took it back to the hotel with me, but didn't eat it then, so figured what the heck, took it home and put it in the freezer.

Same thing with Game 4 in St. Louis. That sandwich sits in my freezer, too. Both are labeled—roast beef from Game 7, ham and cheese from Game 4—and await their placement on eBay. Who would ever have thought that a simple roast beef sandwich would buy a year at Yale? But who would have thought the Red Sox would ever win the World Series, either?

# The Morning After

HAD ALAN GREENSPAN BEEN COMMISSIONER OF BASEBALL RATHER than Commissioner of the Federal Reserve Board, he would have described the Red Sox' 2005 season as a "soft landing."

Boston went 95-67, winning just three fewer games than in 2004. As usual, the word "unprecedented" cropped up when describing the Sox' 2005 season. Boston finished in a dead heat for first place in the AL East with the Yankees, but was relegated to second because of a tie-breaker, that tie-breaker being New York's 10-9 edge in the season series. It was the first time in the 104-year history of the American League that two teams finished tied for the top and did not play off.

Sox fans had television and the need to squeeze three rounds of playoffs into the month of October to blame for the second-place finish. Since Boston made the post-season as a Wild Card team anyway, there was no need to take on the Yankees in a 1978 re-enactment.

The Red Sox won the World Series in 2004 coming out of the Wild Card spot, but went nowhere this time. They played the Chicago White Sox in the Division Series and were swept. The very first Chicago batter up in the first inning of Game 1, Scott

Podsednik, was hit by a Matt Clement pitch and the rest of the series was an equal mess.

That the Red Sox lost in the first round was less of a surprise than the fact that they won 95 games in the regular season. Curt Schilling's ankle did not heal quickly after his 2004 miracle in the playoffs and he was unable to be the Number One starter for the entire season, although he pitched both in relief, and out of the rotation, in mediocre fashion. Keith Foulke, who made the play on Edgar Renteria to end the 2004 World Series, was just awful from Opening Day on. He wound up having surgery on both knees by the time the season ended, and by the time the playoffs arrived, 39-year-old Mike Timlin was the closer.

Clement and David Wells were picked up in the off-season to replace Pedro Martinez and Derek Lowe. The new pitchers performed very well for half of the year. Wells, who at 42 became the oldest pitcher ever to throw a complete game for the Red Sox, had a fine season, period. Clement, who won the unofficial "Player You'd Most Like as Your Next Door Neighbor Award" was a mid-season All-Star, but faltered very badly in the second half and by season's end was a liability. Mark Bellhorn, an unlikely hero in 2004 at second base, spent the first half of 2005 striking out more than a Republican at a Labor Day picnic and was released late in the summer.

After making the final out of the World Series, Renteria signed with Boston in the off-season, replacing Orlando Cabrera, whom the Red Sox let escape to Anaheim via free agency. It was a mistake. Renteria led Boston in both errors and runners stranded in scoring position. Cabrera led the Angels to the AL West title.

Still, the Red Sox led their division for almost the entire summer. In mid-June they went on a 12-1 run to move into first. In late July they started a surge that saw them go 14-2 and build a 5 ½ game lead over the Yankees. But New York caught Boston in the final few days of the season and clinched the division crown at Fenway Park on the next-to-last day. It was a surprise to almost everyone, thanks to a convoluted system of breaking playoff ties in which the Red Sox actually wanted the Indians, a team they had to beat to make the playoffs, to win instead of lose. The scenario of New York clinching the AL East without a playoff with the Red Sox was so far-fetched that nobody anticipated it, and even most Yankees players were aware that they were on the verge of capturing first place until about the eighth inning of the game they did it in.

As usual, there was a Manny Ramirez controversy. He went through his standard Lost in Space routine in the middle of the season and asked to be traded, which of course was next to impossible because of the size of his contract. The Sox kept him, he publicly recanted his trade desires, then went on to finish off what was probably the second best season he had ever had with the bat.

His teammate, David Ortiz, had one of the best seasons any Red Sox hitter had ever had, not just in quantity of production, but in quality. Ortiz won game after game with timely hits in the late innings. In terms of clutch, it was more than Ted Williams had ever done, and it was Carl Yastrzemski, September 1967, only for Ortiz, every month was September 1967.

After the World Series, Johnny Damon published a book called *Idiot*, which is what he had named the 2004 Red Sox during the summer of their charge to the World Series. With a book under his belt, Damon got off to a tremendous start and as September approached was a candidate for American League Most Valuable Player. But. injuries caught up with him and derailed that candidacy.

In June, in Cleveland, the always-approachable Damon was asked to sign a copy of his book for my wife, a big fan. He was glad to do it, and asked that I leave it on his chair in the visitors clubhouse at Jacobs Field, which I did. After 20 minutes of talking with manager Terry Francona, I went back into the clubhouse and there was Damon, sitting in his chair, reading his own book. And not just reading it, but laughing like crazy as he did. He must love to cook for himself, too.

Damon eventually put the book down long enough to sign it, then went out and had a 2 for 5 day with a homer, 2 RBIs and 2 runs scored. Damon might not have wound up as Most Valuable Player, but he was definitely Boston's Most Valuable Author.

While the year ended with the Red Sox being swept in a playoff series for the first time since 1995, it also ended with Boston having its best influx of young talent in even longer than that. Rookie pitcher Jonathan Papelbon was dominating after being called up from the minors late in the season and another rookie pitcher, Craig Hansen, became the first Boston player ever to make his big-league debut in the same year he was drafted.

The Sox brought up pitchers Abe Alvarez and Manny Delcarmen, and finished the regular season with prize prospect Hanley Ramirez on the bench, getting a taste of major-league cuisine.

Since Boston's domination of baseball ended in 1918, the Sox had traditionally followed their rare World Series appearances with dismal day-afters. The 1947 season was lousy, as were 1968, 1976 and 1987. With Papelbon on the mound, and kids like Hansen and Hanley Ramirez on the taxi squad, the 2005 Red Sox were short on victories in the playoffs, but hardly short on hope for more memorable seasons down the line.